The Social Construction of Capabilities in a Tamil Village

The Social Construction of Capabilities in a Tamil Village

L. N. Venkataraman

With a Foreword by

William A. Jackson

Orient BlackSwan

THE SOCIAL CONSTRUCTION OF CAPABILITIES
IN A TAMIL VILLAGE

ORIENT BLACKSWAN PRIVATE LIMITED

Registered Office
3-6-752 Himayatnagar, Hyderabad 500 029, Telangana, India
e-mail: centraloffice@orientblackswan.com

Other Offices
Bengaluru, Chennai, Guwahati, Hyderabad,
Kolkata, Mumbai, New Delhi,
Noida, Patna, Visakhapatnam

First published by Orient Blackswan Private Limited 2021

ISBN 978-81-948295-9-1

Typeset in
Goudy Old Style 10.5/12.6
by Le Studio Graphique, Gurgaon 122 007

032569

Printed in India at
Akash Press, New Delhi 110 020

Published by
Orient Blackswan Private Limited
3-6-752 Himayatnagar, Hyderabad 500 029, Telangana, India
e-mail: info@orientblackswan.com

To
Professor Hans-Uwe Otto

Contents

Abbreviations

AP	Adaptive preferences
BA	Bachelor of Arts
BBA	Bachelor of Business Administration
B.Com	Bachelor of Commerce
B.Ed	Bachelor of Education
BC	Backward Classes
B.PEd	Bachelors in Physical Education
B.Sc	Bachelor of Science
CA	Capabilities approach
CBA	Cost-benefit analysis
CCE	Caste, class and education
CCP	Caste, class and power
DCA	Diploma in Computer Application
D.Coop	Diploma in Cooperative Management
DME	Diploma in Mechanical Engineering
EFA	Education for All
EU	Educated unemployed
EUE	Educated underemployment
EUEY	Educated underemployed youths
EUY	Educated unemployed youths
GNP	Gross national product
HCA	Human capital approach
HD	Human development
HDI	Human Development Index
HPI	Human Poverty Index
IT	Information technology
ITI	Industrial Training Institute

MA	Master of Arts
MBC	Most Backward Classes
M.Com	Master of Commerce
M.Sc	Master of Science
M.Phil	Master of Philosophy
MSW	Masters in Social Work
NSS	National Sample Survey
OBC	Other Backward Classes
PG	Postgraduate
PGD	Postgraduate Diploma
RoR	Rate of returns
SC	Scheduled Castes
SCoC	Social construction of capabilities
SSA	Sarva Shiksha Abhiyan
SSLC	Secondary School Leaving Certificate
ST	Scheduled Tribes
UNDP	United Nations Development Programme
VEC	Village education committee

Tables, Figures and Annexures

Tables

Figures

Annexures

Foreword

Amartya Sen's capability approach offers a rich account of welfare that avoids the narrowness of purely material, monetary or psychological approaches. It stresses a person's ability to do things within a social setting and values the freedom to exercise choice over these activities. Welfare analysis can be opened out and moved beyond measurement along a single abstract dimension. Yet, the capability approach still has weaknesses. Because it is defined in individual terms, it may struggle to capture the true extent of social, cultural and structural influences. It may highlight the internal aspect of capabilities, rather than the external aspect. Unless handled carefully, it may underestimate the importance of culture and society in capability formation, reducing capabilities to synonyms for individual knowledge and skills.

The present book by L. N. Venkataraman eludes any such dangers. From the outset, capabilities are viewed as being socially constructed and not solely a trait of the individual. They cannot be separated from the wider social context: any attempt to do so, in the hope of simplifying the analysis, will damage our understanding. Only by making the effort to interpret the social setting can we grasp how capabilities are formed and how they might be enhanced. The methods adopted here are precisely what are needed in a socially sensitive application of the capability approach. Future researchers would be wise to follow suit. Two key strengths of the book stand out.

First, it brings to the fore the many dimensions that should be recognised. Its conceptual basis draws upon intersectionality, whereby various social identities and positions may interact and cut across each other in a complex fashion. While dimensions such as class, caste and gender will frequently be correlated, they can nevertheless vary independently to yield intricate outcomes. Any individual person will have multiple identities, whose interplay bears upon capabilities. Advantages in some dimensions will not necessarily be matched by advantages in others. Knowledge and skills may be wasted if the social context is unfavourable for their use. In order to comprehend capabilities, we must consider the full range of identities and how they interact.

Second, unlike much welfare literature, the book includes empirical work to illustrate why its ideas have practical relevance. The case study is well chosen. India, with its caste system now being challenged by the forces of economic development, supplies a prime example of tensions among several social and economic dimensions. Selecting a village scrutinised by previous research is illuminating, as it demonstrates the novelty of an intersectional perspective. The author carries out a deep ethnographic assessment aimed at interpreting people's social experiences, with findings detailed enough to escape the bland generalisations often seen in welfare discussion. Despite the localised nature of the case study, the results have broad significance. Similar issues of intersectionality will beset the formation of capabilities in any country or region, developed or less developed. The same interpretative methods will be required at any time or place.

Policymakers who really want to improve capabilities should heed the arguments in this book. There can neither be a quick economic fix from growth alone, nor an easy social policy solution implemented from above: slow, steady social and cultural change will secure the largest gains. To maintain progress and remove the cultural blockages to capabilities, we will have to be aware of the intersectionalities and their effects. Disentangling the complex web of multiple, conflicting identities will not be straightforward, but a starting point is to be conscious of the difficulties. This book is indispensable in delineating the barriers to capability formation and showing how they might eventually be overcome.

William A. Jackson
University of York, UK

Publishers' Acknowledgements

For granting permission to reproduce copyrighted material in this volume, the publishers wish to make the following acknowledgements.

Taylor & Francis, for 'Intersectional Implications of Capabilities Formation'. Originally published as 'Social Construction of Capabilities and Intersectional Complexities in a Tamil Village', *Development in Practice* 25 (8), November 2015: 1170–81. Reprinted with permission of Taylor & Francis.

ASIEN, for 'Education Quality, Employability and Capabilities'. Originally published as 'Quality, Employability and Capabilities: The Enduring Elusive Triangle in Indian Education', *ASIEN: The German Journal on Contemporary Asia* 127, April 2013: S30–47.

SAGE Publishing, for 'Poverty and Education in Sripuram'. Originally published partially as 'Orphan-schooling in India: A Reflexive Account from Sripuram', *Sociological Bulletin: Journal of the Indian Sociological Society* 63 (2), May–August 2014: 302–13.

Informa UK Limited, for 'Capitals and Capabilities'. Originally published as 'Capitals and Capabilities: Social Reproduction of Inequalities in Sripuram', in *Youth, Gender and the Capabilities Approach to Development: Rethinking Opportunities and Agency from a Human Development Perspective*, ed. Aurora Lopez-Fogues and Firdevs Melis Cin, 92–107 (London and New York: Routledge, 2018). Reproduced with permission through PLSclear.

Acknowledgements

This book is based on my D.Phil study on a classical field site in Tamil Nadu. In Social Anthropology, it is often called a *re-study*. I revisited Sripuram with Professor André Béteille's modified framework. I was aware of the pitfalls of trying to step into the master's shoes; I am in regular contact with him for academic consultations. This includes our meetings both in his office at the University of Delhi as well as at his residence in New Delhi; my regular telephonic communications with him have altogether guided me in both my thesis and this book. For all these reasons, I wholeheartedly acknowledge his valuable role.

Like many students of the Social Sciences, I too am influenced by Marx and Weber. I have also developed a keen interest in developmental issues mainly through sociological lenses. This introduced me to Amartya Sen's scholarly works on capabilities, where he has been critical of economic determinism despite being an economist. My continuous engagements with the capabilities approach have inculcated in me a sense of freedom, which was nurtured primarily by my supervisor Professor Hans-Uwe Otto during my project years at the Research School Education and Capabilities (EduCap). His regular suggestions have instilled the necessary confidence in me. I record my gratitude to him. My discussions with him over his kind offerings at the Universität further nurtured my ideas. I immensely value his helpful inputs beyond my research project. Though there might be errors, mainly because of my personal limitations, the merits of my arguments have been strengthened by the academic inputs of Professor Holger Ziegler. He has been generous in giving me patient hearings in Bielefeld.

Besides, I wish to acknowledge my mentors Professor Melanie Walker with whom I had two wonderful years in Bloemfontein, and Professor Dipankar Gupta, for their kind endorsements of this book.

I would also like to thank William Jackson for writing the Foreword. In addition, my interactions with various colleagues have shaped my work into the present form. I wish to acknowledge them for their kindness. They include A. R. Vasavi; Ananta Giri; Andre Keet; Anil Sadgopal; Avanish Kumar; Avinash K. Singh; Bénédicte Zimmermann; Caesar Basu; Chris Fuller; David Clark; Dennis Beach; Des Gasper; Elaine Unterhalter; Isabell Diehm; Jacob Kornbeck; J. B. G. Tilak; Jean-Michael Bonvin; Joanna Pfaff-Czarnecka; Krishna Kumar; Mari-Anne Okkolin; Martha Nussbaum; Merridy Wilson-Strydom; Michael Meuser; Michael Watts; N. Jayaram; Naveen Dubey; Oliver Mutanga; Peter Vale; Pramila Menon; Pulapre Balakrishnan; R. Govinda; Ramachandra Guha; Sabine Andresen; Sabine Schafer; Samuel Fongwa; Sonja Loots; Srinivasan Ramani; Sudhanshu Bhushan; Suresh Babu; Thomas Faist; Uta Quasthoff-Hartmann; Venkatesh Athreya; Venkat Narayanan; Venkatesh Athreya; Vinay Srivastava; Vishal Narain; Vivek; and Wolfgang Max Böttcher.

I have been very fortunate to have friends and colleagues with whom I have had instructive conversations. I wish to mention the 'The Best-Team': Anika Duveneck; Antje Brock; Antoanneta Potsi; Bettina Ritter; Branislava Bosnjak; Daniel Rebbe; Davina Gateley Said; Erika Bozzato; Joshua Eshuchi; Ksenia Kuzmina; Lukas Ertl; Maria Ron Balsera; Rada Jancic; Sittipan Yotyodying; and Zoe Clark. My sincere thanks to them for their kind support during my stay at EduCap.

I also wish to thank the Universität Bielefeld, and the library administration and other officials, in supporting my efforts on this project. Apart from the wonderful library staff, I have the support staff at the Research School to thank. My heartfelt gratitude to Andreas Hoffmann; Anne Klosener; Claudia Dietz; Helga Lehmann; Kirstin Hubeny; Maren R. Eikerling; Patricia Moller-Reusch; and Veronica Horbach.

I am thankful for all the comments I received at various conferences, which gave additional inputs to the sustained suggestions of my Doktorväter; I record my gratitude to the generous financial support of EduCap in allowing me to share my research at prestigious conferences over the years. I also benefitted greatly from the critiques of my students at the Universität Bielefeld. I would like to acknowledge my interactions with Nicole Fliege; Kerstin Hollmann; and Ariane

Olsson. For bringing these precious people in my academic life, my sincere thanks to Professor Isabell Diehm; Kristina Schroder and Susanne Munley for offering me the position of an Affiliated Lecturer in their working group in the Universität Bielefeld. My sincere thanks also to Dr Lucyna Darowska and her colleagues at the International Office for the DAAD Scholarship, which financially supported me during the last phase of this project.

My academic interactions with Masters in Public Policy and SDP students have been a blessing in disguise as they helped test all my perspectives. For this I am grateful to the colleagues at TERI School of Advanced Studies, especially to the vice-chancellor, Professor Manipadma Datta, for all the academic resources offered to me. In addition, I thank my colleagues Rajiv Seth; Shiju; Chaitanya; Vishal; and Ratan Jha. My special gratitude to my inspiring students Abhishek Toppo; Ajmal Behmanish; Ashmeet Kaur; Aynalem; Deepak Virmani Ji; Harsh Jaiswal; Kala Bada; KhaibarTagge; Khamp; Sahil Patni; Sakshi Nigam; Sanchi Jain; Sarvesh Ji; Tesfaye; and Uttara.

My discontinued work on an ambitious multi-sited ethnographic research project in NIEPA taught me valuable lessons. Though these lessons are hard to express in words, my sincere thanks go to Professor Aarti Srivastava for her friendly guidance. In this regard, I also appreciate the role of my friends: Ajay Choubey; Ajith Kannna; Beryl Anand; Bharath Rout; Kannan; Kavitha; M. Mayilvaganan; Nitesh Parashar; Nivedita; P. Sundar; R. Sivakumar; Raj Kumar; Raja Ganesh; Ram; Ramprasad Srivats; Selvaraj; Sudhanshu Patra; and Varadharajan, who immensely supported my theoretical 'trials' and scholastic 'struggles'. It is impossible for me to express my gratitude adequately to the people of Sripuram who have been anonymised for ethnographic reasons. Also, I would record my sincere thanks to my editor Roopa Sharma and Insiya Poonawala of Orient BlackSwan.

Finally, my exceptional gratitude goes to my family: Punam; Rishi; Anu; Balaji; Gayathri; Lallu; Neelamma; Raghuram; Sundararajan; G. Vasudevan; and the inspiring bunch: Akshaya; Bhargav; Ganeshram; Sudha; and Keshav, for bearing my continuous contemplations and my missing of life events in one way or another.

Laksh

one

Introduction

India, an ethnographic 'museum', takes pride in its national notion of unity in diversity. It is a mosaic of religions and castes ordained by various social hierarchies. Unlike many other countries, in India, class is not the sole arbiter of a person's socio-economic reality, and intersectional variables such as caste play a prominent role.

The stratification of a social system based on caste places individuals hierarchically. Inheritance based on birth within a caste structure often provides a 'fixed' identity where social mobility is discouraged. In India, social stratification is based on ascriptive status. Inheritance based on ascription prefers a few at the top of the hierarchy, where they often enjoy socio-economic privileges. The broad classification of *varnashrama dharma*, for instance, stratifies people as Brahmins, Kshatriyas, Vaishyas and Shudras. This ascriptive social order based on the Hindu scriptures places Brahmins (or the 'higher' castes) above others; Kshatriyas, traditionally known for martial valour and managerial roles, are next in the social stratification; Vaishyas, known for trade and commercial activities, are above the last layer of the 'lower' castes. In this fourfold ascriptive division of labour, the 'lower' castes are often addressed as Shudras (or Dalits or Harijans). The ascriptive nature of the caste system in India is, thus, unique where social status is mostly determined by birth.[1]

The intersection between caste and economic variables often re/produces the 'underclass' (MacDonald 1997). As caste-specific sociological depiction has been well-established in mainstream literature, the present study uses the framework of the social construction of capabilities (SCoC)[2] to analyse the intersections of caste, class and education. This intersectionality is conceptualised to understand the social construction of 'mutually constitutive relations among social identities' (Shields 2008: 301).

The central analysis of the social construction of capabilities approach is based on ethnographic fieldwork conducted in a south Indian village pseudonymously named Sripuram. Renowned Indian sociologist André Béteille studied this village in the 1960s, conducting social anthropological fieldwork on the caste, class and power (CCP) dimensions (Béteille 1965a). The present work attempts to analyse caste, class and education (CCE) by revisiting the same village after five decades. As the research has been conceptually influenced by the capabilities approach (Sen 1999b), its primary aim is to highlight the complex interactions of human agency and social structure.[3] Based on ethnographic fieldwork, it examines the role of education across diverse social groups, including among the educated un/underemployed youth as well as deprived children in the village. Observations of everyday interactions and coping strategies of the poor in their socio-economic spheres have provided valuable insights into both education and poverty in Sripuram. The social construction of capabilities analysis thus highlights the issues of capabilities and functionings formations of the poor in Tamil Nadu, which have larger implications for understanding the correspondence between the rising un/underemployment and the inferior educational provisioning of the Indian state.

The concept of intersectionality as 'a complex system assumes a methodology that sees everything as interactions, not "main effects"' (Choo and Ferree 2010: 136). It highlights the intangible structural factors in the educational outcomes of a given subject community. The intersectional analysis, thus, successfully offers 'insights missed in even excellent sociological work' (ibid.: 130). This is critical in the present context as the acclaimed sociological works of M. N. Srinivas and Béteille have somehow overlooked the intersectional dimensions in their contributions on India,[4] although this limitation has not been a conscious self-restriction on the scholars' parts. While one must acknowledge the emerging current interest in intersectional research studies, methodologically, intersectionality studies are yet to capture the attention of mainstream research. The present work underlines their significance, given the complex reality of India as one of the most stratified societies in the world.

Situating Sripuram

Though for ethnographic reasons of anonymity Sripuram is a pseudonymously given name, André Béteille shared the exact location of the village with the author while introducing him to it. Sripuram, a small village in Tanjore district, is located on the banks of river Kaveri in the south Indian state of Tamil Nadu. Béteille's oft-cited *Caste, Class and Power* (1965a)–one of the critical sociological texts on India–is based on his study of this multi-caste village.

Like any other Tamil village, Sripuram is inhabited by diverse socio-economic groups where the presence of various castes is visible. The village is divided into many streets, mainly along caste lines. For instance, the Agraharam, where Brahmins or the erstwhile 'higher' castes live, is the first street that anyone entering the village will come across. This is parallel to other streets where villagers of different social groups live. The Other Backward Classes (OBC), often called Dominant Castes in the literature (Srinivas 1987), live in the streets adjacent to the Agraharam.[5] The OBCs in the village are a conglomeration of diverse caste groups, including the Kallars, Padayachis and Vellalars. Socio-economically they occupy the middle layer between the Brahmins and the Pallars. Historically, the latter occupied the lower rung of physical as well as social hierarchies, and are often addressed in the village as Scheduled Castes (SCs) or Dalits. Their past socio-economic position seems to be the main reason for their present deprivation. They represent almost all indicators of ill-being, such as economic deprivation, illiteracy, unemployment and educated underemployment in the village.

The presence of these three broad social groups highlights remarkably different lifestyles. Even though the OBCs and Pallars might look identical to outsiders, one can observe subtler forms of social unrest. This unrest often displays primordial identities. In contrast, one can notice the in/voluntary social distancing of the Brahmins from the 'others' in the village. The Brahmins of Sripuram, like those elsewhere in the country, are known for their cultural capital, as they have historically occupied the echelons of power. They owned most of the land in the village until a few decades ago. Béteille (1965a: 15) has often referred to them as Mirasdars, or landowners. The ownership of land gave the Brahmins the power to control others who were economically dependent on these landholdings. Their social position as a 'higher' caste has allowed them to enhance their cultural capital over the years.[6] The intersection of socio-economic and educational factors has naturally ensured their growth and development. As an illustration, Brahmin women are often more highly educated and knowledgeable than men of other castes in the village. This contrasts with the general presumption that women, across castes, occupy the lower rungs of the patriarchy.

Against this backdrop, revisiting the Béteillean framework of CCP with a new outline of CCE convinced the author to provide a reflexive account of the intersection of human capital ideals and social capital influences on capabilities formation.[7] The ethnographic research offers deep insights into an understanding of the social construction of functionings and capabilities. This is especially observed in light of the 'invisible contestation' in the caste system because of diminishing economic and social opportunities.[8] This is further reinforced in the social order as the economic success of any caste is primarily determined by its employment outcome. Almost all caste groups treat education as an instrumentalist notion of human capital. This clearly goes against any scholastic attempt to understand education in terms of capabilities. Even their employment-centric approaches do not assure them of any economic avenues. This underscores the social reproduction of inequalities in Sripuram.[9]

Considering this instrumentalism, ethnographic visits to the local school and orphanage underline the fact that the institutionalised welfare structures, with their poor learning outcomes, are re/producing the deprivation trap in the village. The reflexive analyses from the fieldwork have further brought out the fact that the children's well-being is mainly dependent on their institutional presence and human agency in the social structure. These children, in turn, receive 'ill-being'[10] due to their position in the social structure as well as the hierarchy of stratification in the village.[11] Also, their everyday life is at the institutional margins due to infrastructural inadequacies of the orphanage as well as the mediocre educational quality of the local school. Given these cumulative disadvantages, neither the broader notions of capabilities nor the narrower definitions of functionings is proximate to their agential well-being in Sripuram.[12]

By consolidating theoretical as well as conceptual insights on education and development, one can understand the complexities of social change. This is possible because of the sustained interaction among diverse sociological factors. One can appreciate this complexity because of readings of the latest research paradigms such as the capabilities approach. This is crucial, as social reality is an elusive phenomenon which one analyses either through structural constraints or agential aspirations. In contrast, this work analyses the dualism between them. The differential educational outcomes of social groups have further been conceptualised based on systemic segregations along socio-economic differences. As this segregation questions the very notions of social justice, it is critical to note that the poor are often left with government schools, which are notorious for their lack of quality. This is conceptually crucial because 'with adequate social opportunities, individuals can effectively shape their destiny and help each other' (Sen 1999b: 11). In addition to a discussion of educational deprivations, the central objective here is an analysis of the functionings and failures of the educated unemployed and underemployed youth in Sripuram. The adaptive preferences[13] and coping strategies of these youths in the informal economy in Meenakshipuram as well as in Sripuram underline the dysfunctional complexities[14] in the social construction of capabilities (Venkataraman 2018b).[15] In this social construction, the current analysis underscores how the intersectionality of caste and class plays an intricate role in shaping education and employment in the dynamics of capabilities formation in Sripuram.

The Background

Historically, every developed society has been largely literate. In contrast, almost all illiterate societies are poor in their social development indicators. Though this historical-social fact has highlighted the intrinsic link between education and development, there are relatively few works of sociological research available on educational outcomes.[16] Further, the impact of intersectional effects on outcome analyses is an under-researched domain. Intersectionality, which may be defined as 'the mutually constitutive relations among social identities' (Shields 2008: 301), is a unique reality in India where society is not simply based on class dynamics as in other parts of the world. The caste system with its class dynamics bestows on India the dubious distinction of being one of the most highly stratified societies in the world, where hierarchy is based on an ascriptive division of labour. According to this, primordial identities intersecting across a complex set of socio-economic factors place individuals in different social positions. This intersectional 'uniqueness' of caste and class across ascription and achievement has been well documented by Gough (1981: 136): 'India is a peripheral segment of the (changing) world capitalist system, which is characterized by a single, although changing, mode of production and forms a single, although changing, social formation, there being only one of it in the world.'

Also, the political economy of India is complex. For instance, in contrast to the popular developmental rhetoric of the trickle-down effect, it has been found that 'the years of high economic growth were not accompanied by a spurt in employment generation and rise in average earnings of the workforce' (Breman 2010: 43). Due to this, the space for public institutions has shrunk as the poor are pushed to bond 'only by primordial loyalties such as caste, ethnicity and religion' (ibid.: 46). The result is the re/production of the social status quo in the country. This newer social formation needs to be understood as India has some of the most impoverished individuals in the world, and the majority of them live in rural areas (Ayres and Simon 2003: 211).

These newer formations could certainly be observed in the states where 'high urbanisation and modern industrialisation seem to show a rather poor record in poverty reduction' (Kannan and Raveendran 2011: 62). The case of Tamil Nadu must be mentioned as an example. Its record in reducing the incidence of poverty—as officially defined—is quite impressive. However, 'it has an incidence of poverty and vulnerability at around 73%' (ibid.). Although Tamil Nadu has been known for its economic dynamism over the years, it has been performing poorly with regard to social inclusion and equality (ibid.: 69). In their measurement of poverty and vulnerability, Kannan and Raveendran conclude that Tamil Nadu has the highest inequality in India (ibid.: 64).

Considering this complex socio-economic reality, the present framework underlines the necessity of studying the social construction of capabilities in Tamil Nadu.[17] For this, it conceptualises educational outcomes of the poor as its central concern.[18] 'Educational outcome', in the sociological sense, is not just an end product, which is generally understood as completion or achievement expressed in the form of data. Rather, the present work also understands educational outcome as the process of learning in terms of the theoretical notion of functionings. It must be noted that the concept of 'functionings' has been defined extensively in the capabilities approach. For instance, Nussbaum (2011: 25) has defined it as 'beings and doings that are the outgrowths or realizations of capabilities'. Since functionings and capabilities together form the central tenets of the capabilities approach, it is important to know the interlinkages between the two. Functionings 'are the outcomes or achievements, whereas capabilities are the real opportunities to achieve valuable states of being and doing' (Robeyns 2006: 78).

Against this background, this work treats capabilities formation as the intersectionality of social factors in the country. In India, capabilities formation is conditioned mainly by two crucial factors: the intersectional aspects of caste–class dynamics in the immediate local context; and in the wider socio-economic contexts where 'external' forces come into play. In this context, Jean Drèze's (2004b: 354) analysis has established that literacy achievements in India 'depend crucially on the social context: the gender division of labour, the kinship system, caste-related norms, economic entitlements, and so on'. Thus, intersectional aspects of caste and class dynamics are crucial in the country, and Sripuram represents one such social reality.

The conceptual framework for this study has been broadly motivated by three ethnographic concerns: (i) Is poverty the single variable in determining educational outcomes for the poor in Sripuram?[19] If so, (ii) what kinds of capabilities do the poor acquire through education? And, (iii) what is the role of social capital in educational outcomes of the poor across different castes in the village?[20] These three concerns have been approached so as to highlight the interactions of caste–class dynamics in education and to show how intersectionality informs and is reflected in the relationship between educational attainment and socio-economic conditions of the poor among different castes in Sripuram.

Thus, the central analysis aims to understand how educational functionings impact occupations as well as other domains of life, while attempting to underline the complexities of caste, class and education in Sripuram. Theoretical strands of the capabilities approach have been consulted to aid this analysis. To collect thick descriptions and reflexive[21] insights, the author undertook ethnographic fieldwork in Sripuram in phases between 2008 and 2012, the details of which are presented in the following chapters. The motivation for the present work is based on established necessities of the literature where 'more information is needed on how family economic circumstances and processes' impact educational outcomes (Banerji 1997: 2058). It was important to understand the intrinsic complexities in the relationship between education and development, especially because educational outcomes—at least regarding occupations—are neither automatic nor uniform across diverse groups in any society.

Tanjore: The Context

The district of Tanjore, or Thanjavur, in Tamil Nadu is famous for its temples and Carnatic music. Also known for its fertile soils and vast areas under wet paddy cultivation, it is popularly called the granary of south India (Sivertsen 1963: 14). As Tanjore district owes much of its historical and contemporary significance to its physical characteristics (Béteille 1972a: 126), it offers certain advantages 'for the investigations of agrarian relations as an aspect of the broader problem of social stratification. It displays extremes of inequality regarding both caste and class and a close, though changing relationship between the two' (ibid.: 124). A study of Tanjore is, thus, relevant to observe how caste helps or hinders educational outcomes along class lines. Tanjore is also interesting because of the changes in its landownership patterns, following the exodus and the absentee-landlordism of the Brahmins. Furthermore, Sripuram displays the continuing socio-economic reality of Tanjore's old order, where a large part of the workforce consists of agricultural labour, 'of whom again the scheduled castes form a very high proportion' (Guhan 1984: 210). This is further contextualised by an economic reality where 'colonial rule and capitalist development led to economic stagnation and poverty in Thanjavur' (Washbrook 1983: 567).

Revisiting the Classic

In his review of Béteille's *Caste, Class and Power*, Nandy (1966: 730) considered Sripuram a 'well-selected village community' undergoing rapid and radical change often driven by diverse social processes and intersectional dynamics, whereby the village becomes part of a much broader economic system, primarily because 'class has attained a far greater measure of autonomy in relation to caste' (Chauhan 1967: 1120).

This village, known for its ancient religious and cultural heritage, lies about 8 miles north of Tanjore city, along the sacred northern bank of the river Kaveri. In Béteille's (2009a: 20–22) description, the river has a twofold significance in the lives of the villagers: 'It provides a copious supply of water for irrigation, and it is ranked high among the rivers by Hindus. Brahmins, particularly, prefer to live close to the river because religious merit is acquired by performing the daily Sandhya rites on the waters of the Kaveri.'[22] Today, the flow of the river is determined by the political dynamics between Tamil Nadu and neighbouring Karnataka, the state where it originates.

The physical structure of the village reflects its social stratification: the Agraharam is inhabited by Brahmins, the Kudiana by non-Brahmins, and the Cheri by the Adi-Dravidas. Though the residential settlement pattern shows conspicuous features of segregation among castes even today, Béteille's work underlines the nature of 'caste fusions between proximate segments [that] have occurred due to secularization and westernization' (Sinha 1973: 294). The current nature of change is remarkably different from that seen in earlier sociological descriptions of Sripuram.[23] For instance, the Agraharam is no longer the exclusive residential street for Brahmins, and has seen the entry of non-Brahmins and OBCs over the years. This change has been possible partly due to the large-scale exodus of Brahmins from the village for economic reasons. Thus, the Béteillian description of Sripuram as an Agraharam village or a Brahmin village (Béteille 1965b: 76) is no longer a social reality today; the exodus of Brahmins and their replacement with non-Brahmins presents the new reality. Also, in Béteille's terminology, the Kudiana is an inclusive name for the streets where non-Brahmins live in Sripuram. Today, the Kudiana comprises seven streets,[24] and is no longer a single residential unit. Contrary to the significant changes in the Agraharam and Kudiana, the Cheri, where the Adi-Dravidas live, is still exclusively meant for the Pallars.[25]

In his earlier work, Béteille had categorised the caste composition of the village into Brahmin, non-Brahmin and Adi-Dravida (Pallar). Distinctive styles of living have also characterised these three segments, often expressed in ritual terms (ibid.). Though there is no visible change even today in the caste scheme as described by Béteille, one can observe changes in the categorisation of social class. According to Béteille's description, the threefold caste blocs in the 1960s generally corresponded to the three principal economic classes, namely the landowners (who were predominantly Brahmin), the tenants (non-Brahmins) and the labourers (Pallars). Today, one can find changes in this scheme, which have been wrought mainly by education. Over the years, the Brahmins have given up their absentee-landlordism due to socio-economic as well as educational factors. There is now a departure from the original scheme—the new landowners, or neo-Mirasdars, are predominantly non-Brahmins. Though most of the Pallars are still dependent on these neo-Mirasdars, education has played a significant role in this change.

While Béteille's descriptions of the settlement pattern of the villagers are relevant even today, some modifications are required. The nomenclature of the threefold classification of castes needs to change. For example, in this work, the non-Brahmins, as a cluster of castes in the middle layer, have been addressed either as the Dominant Castes (see Srinivas 1987) or, as in official terminology, as OBCs.[26] The way in which one addresses a caste by name has also changed due to the broader political economy in Tamil Nadu.[27] For instance, before Béteille's fieldwork, the present-day Dalits in Sripuram were addressed as Pallan. The political structure at the time of Béteille's fieldwork addressed them as Palla, and he also addresses them as such. However, today they must be addressed 'with respect', as Pallar, the difference lying in the progressive renaming of the caste. Anyone using the earlier nomenclature of Pallan or Palla may be censured or even legally challenged.

THE AGRARIAN SOCIAL STRUCTURE

In Asia, a majority of the people live in villages. Ishwaran (1970a: 1), for instance, affirms that the battle for free Asia is being fought in the villages.[28] According to the 2011 Census figures, nearly 70 per cent of the people in India live in villages.[29] Though this justifies the necessity for sociological research on rural social structure, the high noon of 'village studies' in India passed quite some time ago (Madan 1984: 388). This is mainly due to the failure of Indian sociology, which is of relatively recent origin, to develop a tradition of its own (Béteille 1974: 7). In this scenario, any attempt to study social change in the lives of the poor through education would understandably be challenging. However, countering this challenge is necessary because India has some of the poorest people in the world, the majority of whom live in rural areas (Ayres and Simon 2003: 211). This requires intensive field studies of village life to 'map the morphology and content of social change in wider terms' (Ishwaran 1970a: 2). It is against this backdrop that the author undertook ethnographic fieldwork between the years 2008 and 2012 in Sripuram.

As 'each field study of a village cannot be understood except as part of a complex system of coordinates' (ibid.: 6), today a village has become part of a much broader economic system where class positions are increasingly aligned along caste lines. The combination of these two axes, caste and class, is central in determining the quality of rural life. Agrarian relations are thus influenced not only by considerations of inherited status, but also by impersonal market forces and legislation (Nandy 1966: 729). The correlation between caste and landownership, for example, is no longer present in Sripuram, the principal landowners mainly being non-Brahmins and, in a few cases, Pallar. There are only two Brahmin landowners in the village today.[30]

As Breman (1974: *xiii*) notes, India has retained the character of a peasant society despite the accelerated process of urbanisation and industrialisation that it has undergone over the past few decades. In peasant society, low castes and 'untouchables' have constituted the majority of landless workers and have lived separated from the high castes for centuries. This is particularly true of the former 'untouchables', who only came into contact with the higher castes on a professional basis (Etienne 1968: 98). Since the exodus of the erstwhile higher castes from agriculture to urban-centric employment today, these regular professional contacts have been disappearing. This, to a greater extent, increases social distance in the village.[31] The functional role of education of the Brahmins and their exclusivist lifestyles are embedded in the distancing process.[32] In this context, Fuller's (2012: *xv*) observation that 'by the end of the century, only a small minority of Tamilnadu's Brahmins still resided in the countryside' acquires significance. The relative effect of this also influences other castes, as education becomes an active agent for emigration. This has urbanised the villagers where the Brahmins, for instance, were 'transformed during the twentieth century from an agrarian class of landlords into an educated, urban middle class, whose employment ranges from well-paid, professional occupations at the upper end to white-collar jobs as clerks or petty bureaucrats, for example, at the lower end' (ibid.: *xix*).

In light of the above, the physical structure of the village is, in some measure, a reflection of its social structure (Béteille 2009b: 19); the changes in the settlement pattern still show the same conspicuous features of residential segregation between castes in Sripuram. In Béteille's words, 'People who are close to each other in the social system tend to live side-by-side; people whose social positions are widely different live apart. Other things being equal, physical distance can be seen as a function of structural distance' (ibid.).

In contrast, the present-day social reality in Sripuram is increasingly changing. One can find a caste-mixing of residential units in the Agraharam. Though this is a structural beginning for potential changes in the future, one can still find the Pallars or Adi-Dravidas only in the Cheri, which is marked by its visible distance from the 'power centres' in Sripuram. The only notable change is in the nomenclature of the Cheri, which is now called Vadakku Theru (North Street). Over the years, education has not brought any qualitative changes, except in the continuous creation of educated un/underemployed youth in the village.[33]

As 'research may generate in a topic by posing an intellectual problem that people had not thought of or had not previously had any interest in' (Hammersley 2003: 35), the present framework attempts to take up some new analytical categories. The central concern is the social construction of capabilities, which is the first of its kind in India.

The present research carries this approach to the classical field site of Sripuram. Moreover, the adoption of a qualitative poverty dimension to identify the poor regarding intersectional analyses adds a significant conceptual flavour to the subject. For these novelties, C. J. Fuller has acknowledged the importance of the present research in his new introduction to Béteille's *Caste, Class and Power*. To quote:

> First and most simply, *CCP*, like other ethnographies of the village studies era, is an important historical source about the social structure of Indian villages in the early decades following Independence. It is therefore invaluable to any scholar seeking to understand developments in Indian rural society over the last half-century, and restudies of villages—including the one now in progress in Sripuram—can make a significant contribution to our understanding of today's rapidly changing India. (Fuller 2012: *xxxi*)

Notes

1. Though this is an inheritance-based division of labour, one can find a complex and layered picture of regional variations across the country. Each layer in the fourfold classification is a conglomeration of diverse caste groups, which often have endogamous rules and regulations. These rules often determine other social aspects, including commensality, even today.

2. Capabilities in this framework means the competence or life skills one learns in the process of education. This definition attempts to understand whether the broader notion of capabilities formation is available to the poor. The importance of capabilities has thus been analysed in light of their effects on the poor's ability to break the cycle of (economic) deprivation and (social) exclusion.

3. 'Social structure' may be defined as a recurrent social pattern or arrangement, which both emerges from and determines the actions of individuals; it influences or limits the choices and opportunities available. The nature of an 'element' in a structure depends on its interrelations with other elements. The notion of 'agency' in this framework refers to the capacity of individuals to act independently and make their own free choices.

4. This has been acknowledged by Béteille in his personal interviews with the author, who has maintained regular correspondence with him since 2008. In Béteille's view, gender as an important dimension has 'slipped out' of the central focus in their works.

5. The Agraharam is also where the Brahmins collectively live, even in the towns of Tamil Nadu. The current social interaction order in Sripuram, however, is more 'democratic' than that of the Béteillean period, as the forthcoming chapters will show.

6. In related accounts of education, Gilbertson (2014) and Venkataraman (2018b) have discussed the ethnographic description of cultural capital in India.

7. According to the literature, while capabilities are the real opportunities to achieve valuable states of being and doing, functionings are the outcomes or achievements (Robeyns 2006: 78).

8. For additional references, see Chapter 6.

9. For similar conceptual arguments see, for instance, Walker (2012).

10. Ill-being refers to the choice constraints faced by the orphan children in the village. This is an expression conceptualised in contrast to the general notion of well-being. This was inspired by Harriss-White's conception of 'illfare' in the context of the welfare rhetoric in India (Harriss-White and Subramanian 1999).

11. For similar arguments, see ibid.

12. For the theoretical nuances of 'disadvantage' along similar lines, see Wolff and de-Shalit (2007).

13. According to the capabilities approach literature, 'adaptive preferences' are self-subordinating beliefs. For details, see Khader (2009) and Teschl and Comim (2005).

14. Dysfunctional complexities refer to the constraints the youths of the village face due to their coping mechanisms arising out of their circumstances.

15. Meenakshipuram is a pseudonymously named small town near Sripuram. It is one of the block headquarters in the Tanjore district. According to the administrative division, Sripuram falls under this small town and its socio-economic activities consequently depend on Meenakshipuram.

16. See, for instance, Aschaffenburg and Maas (1997); DiMaggio (1982); DiMaggio and Mohr (1985); Dumais (2002); Dunne and Gazeley (2008); Ho Sui-Chu and Willims (1996); Katsillis and Rubinson (1990); Kingston (2001); Lamont and Lareau (1988); Lareau and Horvat (1999); Sullivan (2001); and Teachman (1987).

17. Education is defined here as the process of learning the life skills and capabilities an individual or group gains in the formal or non-formal mode, or in both, in a society. As this study aims to understand educational outcomes for the poor across social groups, it considers only the formal mode of learning. As the village under study shows the differential stages and status of education across its diverse social groups, the present work conceptualises education essentially as a socialisation factor in Sripuram.

18. 'Outcome' in this study refers to educational functionings, which broadly include the achievement, significance and completion of education. To understand the significance of education, the author conducted his fieldwork in both the village school and the orphanage. The study also included the educated, un/underemployed youth in Sripuram, as the following chapters show.

19. The central concern is to understand educational outcomes for the poor across social groups through three aspects, namely capabilities, social mobility and social capital. The poor are defined as people or groups who are either economically deprived or socially discriminated, or both, in their livelihood situations in the village. To arrive at this definition, the study considers two crucial factors: the sociological conception of 'relative deprivation'; and the subjective definition of 'poor'. According to relative deprivation, the status of the poor is not simply based on income inadequacies among individuals and groups, but must also be understood in terms of their societal context. The subjective definition, furthermore, is based on people's definitions of their deprivation and social exclusion. These two factors have been combined to identify the poor across all social groups in the village.

20. Social capital is an intangible asset that an individual or group has due to their ascriptive status of being a member of a particular caste or class. In this study, the discussion on social capital gains momentum because of its analysis of the economic and social mobilities of the poor. While migration to nearby towns seems to be the only developmental avenue, the role of social capital is central to intersectionality, as shown in Chapter 7. Also see, for instance, Venkataraman (2018b).

21. Reflexivity is a process of examining the behaviour of the self in relation to others.

22. Brahmins no longer perform the daily *sandhya* rites (at least in public) in Sripuram. For details, see Chapter 8.

23. This is dealt with in detail in Chapter 8.

24. They are: Sivan Koil Theru, Kali Amman Koil Theru, Perumal Koil Theru, Odakkara Theru, Uppukkara Mettu Theru, Pillayar Koil Theru and Kezha Theru. In Tamil, *theru* means street.

25. Pallars are the erstwhile 'lower' castes or 'untouchables' who are today part of the collective social grouping of Dalits, and officially listed under the SCs due to their social and economic backwardness in Tamil Nadu. In Béteille's descriptions, the Pallars are mentioned as Adi-Dravida.

26. 'OBC' is the official terminology of the central government. In the present context, OBCs include the Backward Classes (BC) and the Most Backward Classes (MBC) in Tamil Nadu.

27. According to recent statistics in Tamil Nadu, nearly 70 per cent of the state's total population are OBCs and roughly 23 per cent are SCs. Given this demographic reality where roughly 93 per cent of the total population are non-Brahmins (which includes both OBCs and SCs), one finds broader policy decisions in light of populist demands (see, for instance, Government of India 2011: 253).

28. See Béteille (1972c, 1974); Breman (1974); and Lerche (2010).

29. As per the 2011 Census, 69 per cent of India's population lives in villages.

30. Though both are no longer interested in agriculture, one of them told me he was 'not worried due to his small piece of land to toil'.

31. American sociologist Emory S. Bogardus attempted to empirically measure the degree of closeness among diverse social groups; this is often known as the Bogardus scale.

32. It is pertinent to mention Drèze's (2004b: 345) observation that 'remaining uneducated is almost unthinkable for the Tamil Brahmin'. In the context of Sripuram, the functional roles of education of the Brahmins must be contrasted with the backwardness of the 'others'. This is crucial in case of the Pallars, who are generally the first-generation learners in the village. The result is social distancing due to differential educational outcomes.

33. This is dealt with in detail in the outcome analyses of the poor in the following chapters.

two

The Complexities of Poverty

India is one of the most stratified societies. The caste system with its myriad forms of superordination and subordination, its many customs and taboos, is perhaps responsible for conferring this dubious distinction (Gupta 1991). Aspects of social exclusion arising out of this are often ascriptive in nature. The central insights of the literature reviewed here predominantly underline the role of social structure on the issues of exclusion. They also highlight the absence of sociological works on educational functionings from a capabilities perspective.

Along with this limitation, there are shared traditions through which economists comprehend various indices of human development. This most often hides social differences between diverse groups at the aggregate level, which underscores the need to sociologically understand the capabilities paradigm in a complex social reality like that of India.

This is an important attempt because the inadequacies of the readily available 'analyses' based on quantitative datasets can only be indicators of the social trends in various development reports. Naturally, scholastic comprehension of social reality also calls for qualitative frameworks. Against this backdrop, the present framework intends, on the one hand, to ethnographically understand the social construction of capabilities, and on the other, it attempts to critique the mainstream literature. At a broader level, this attempt is aimed to at identifying the dominant analytical constructs underpinned in different disciplines to find out new paradigms to reflect on the emerging social realities. The existing literature on educational outcomes can broadly be categorised into four types: developmental studies, sociology, economics and interdisciplinary understandings in education. While these subjects with diverse scholastic backgrounds throw light mainly on subaltern issues, the capabilities approach of Amartya Sen is nearly absent. Only recently did Thorat (2007) discuss these issues from the perspective of economics. This review also observed that only a few sociological works (Unterhalter 2003b; Zimmermann 2006) attempt to understand the capabilities approach in education. Although there has been a good volume of research on subaltern studies (Nambissan 2000; Thorat 2005, 2007; Wankhede 2001), the capabilities approach with a sociological framework is almost absent in India. These inadequacies set the background for this book.

Definitional Dilemmas

Definitions of poverty are by and large driven by economic explanations. This is becuase of convenience of measurement—the poverty line, for example, considers the minimum level of income needed for a bare minimum amount of food for survival, and nothing else (Tilak 2002a: 191). This survival-based characterisation, in turn, limits other analytical definitions. Contrary to this designation, Townsend's (1954: 133) subjective characterisation asserts that '... a family is deemed to be in poverty if the joint income of the members, *supposing it were all available and wisely spent*, would not suffice to purchase for them the necessaries of life ...'. This has also been underlined by others such as Levine (2004), who defines poverty as on the opposing pole to freedom. For him, poverty results either when capability does not develop, or when the opportunity to exercise it is unavailable.

This gap between definitions has also been widely acknowledged. In Béteille's (2003) words:

> ... those who adopt the head-count approach favour an absolute conception of poverty and pursue the specific and limited objective of finding out if the number and proportion of the poor as defined according to a fixed standard are decreasing or increasing. Others adopt a relative conception of poverty, mindful of the fact that as societies change, the standards by which poverty is assessed also change. Here, it may be noted as a matter of the fact that the standards rarely move downwards, they generally move upwards. (Ibid.: 4460)

Appreciating the movements of these standards is crucial, as the well-being of the individuals will not simply be based on survival. Hence, the 'official' definition of poverty has theoretically been simplistic, as it arbitrarily puts the people above and below the lines of poverty. In a nutshell, those who study poverty from a sociological or economic perspective in India, as Béteille has rightly argued, have been concerned less with its definition than its measurement (ibid.: 4455). The position against the obsessive empiricism in the definition of poverty has arisen out of Béteille's opposition to economic determinism in the definition. This op/position is justifiable considering the limitation on data collection where people generally avoid giving the exact income figures to strangers.[1] Given the unavailability of income figures where the nature of an economy is 'roughly' arranged in informal work (of the unorganised sector, for instance), people's will to 'not appear shameful in public' has to be underlined. This underscores the urgency to go beyond the economic variables.

Also, understanding this definitional chasm is crucial in the Indian context, as the problem of poverty mostly goes hand in hand with social exclusion. For instance, Sengupta, Raveendran and Kannan (2008: 49) suggest that despite high growth, more than three-fourths of Indians are weak and vulnerable to a level of consumption not more than twice of that of the official poverty line. This proportion of the population, which can be categorised as the 'common people', is much higher among certain social groups, especially among the Scheduled Castes (SC) and Scheduled Tribes (ST). This complexity is mainly because of the social structure which stratifies groups according to their ascriptive status. In this context, the disturbing question of Béteille gains significance: '[A]re poverty and inequality increasing?' The Indian experience in the second half of the twentieth century underlines the difficulty in answering the question even if poverty is defined narrowly in purely economic terms (Béteille 2003: 4457).

The process of social exclusion arises out of the axis of deprivation and exclusion, giving the sociologist scope to observe the analytical categories. However, a significant problem in the study of inequality is to 'identify the spaces and to analyse how they are related to each other through encompassment, exclusion or inclusion' (Béteille 1993: 753). In India, much of the research on poverty since Independence has been driven by concern for growth and development (Béteille 2003: 4457). It soon became clear that development and growth were not the same things. Where growth leads to increases in poverty and inequality, it can hardly be called development in any meaningful sense of the term (ibid.: 4458). This assessment gains significance, as Sen also suggests in *Development as Freedom* (1999b: 108) that the 'policy debates have indeed been distorted by over-emphasis on income poverty and income inequality, to the neglect of deprivations that relate to other variables, such as unemployment, ill-health, lack of education, and social exclusion'. This is in line with Béteille (1993: 755) when he suggests that 'the unequal power, like unequal esteem, is a far deeper source of inequality than unequal income'.

However, there are important caveats which have also been observed in the literature. For instance, Béteille has established that the relationship between poverty and inequality is neither clear nor direct. As poverty and inequality are analytically distinct concepts, he concludes that they vary independently of each other, and it is misleading beyond a point to treat one as a marker of the other (Béteille 2003: 4455). This caution gives scope to the present analysis to adopt the relative conception of deprivation. Furthermore, Béteille underlines that those who use an absolute concept of poverty find it easier to delink poverty and inequality because their main concerns are inequalities of income and expenditure. On the other hand, those who adopt a relative concept of poverty tend to argue that there is a close if not inextricable relationship between inequality and poverty (ibid.: 4456).

This is critical, as absolute poverty persists even in countries that are economically advanced and have little population growth. In Béteille's judgement, this has led sociologists to be sceptical about the assumption of a simple relationship between poverty, inequality and economic backwardness (ibid.: 4457). Hence, social inequality is not just a matter of distribution of goods and resources among individuals, but also one of the relations among persons with a component of evaluation built into them (Béteille 1993: 755). This has become important in adopting a subjective definition of poverty regarding relative deprivations.

Measurement Issues

As discussed earlier, those who study poverty in the Indian context have been concerned less with its definition than its measurement, with economic determinism as the dominant perspective marked by an absence of other diverse perspectives. Against this backdrop, Townsend's (1954: 133) argument for a subjective designation of poverty is essential, as it discusses the social structures of the poor: 'In considering the spending habits of poorer people, it seems that due regard must be paid to the conventions sanctioning membership of their community, to the influence of economic and social measures currently adopted by society.'

Complexities of India's social structure add an extra dimension to the discussion. Although most members of the SCs live in villages, Wankhede's (2001: 1555) assessment, for instance, highlights that the urban-based castes present a positive picture of progress as compared to the rural population when the overall progress is measured. In addition to this complexity, some of the literature complains about a reductionist understanding, which sees education primarily as a 'social safety' measure for countries to protect the disadvantaged from further marginalisation caused by globalisation, and to exploit the skills and knowledge of their domestic workers in the world market (Rampal 2000: 2524). As a result, the present work underlines the need for a comparative perspective in the research.

Thus, when it comes to measurement, it is essential to discuss the perspective of the capabilities approach as it provides a better theoretical grounding. Tilak (2002a) has discussed a conceptual trajectory of the role of the capabilities approach perspective in education, and impressively argued for this approach. To him, the human development approach recognises education primarily not as an instrument or means of development, but as development itself, while the lack of the same is not just a cause of poverty, but poverty itself. Educational deprivation or poverty of education becomes an integral part of human poverty. Accordingly, standard of living, quality of life, human development, human poverty, and so on, are measured with regard to, among other things, the educational status of the population (ibid.: 195). This has further been strengthened by Unterhalter (2003a), who has commented upon the capabilities approach:

> It allows us to look not just at a narrow measure of benefit (usually equated with income) but generates a wider range of insights about what participants value and how achieving short-term functionings relate to wider concerns with capabilities. These

> encompass not just capabilities about a project but in relation to society. (Alkire 2002: 281, as quoted in Unterhalter 2003a: 668)

Moreover, it is essential to contextualise the argument by Walker and Unterhalter (2007: 250) here: '... it is evident that enrolment is not a useful measure of whether people learn and that the many different interpretations of literacy make this a particularly imprecise indicator of knowledge and capacity to engage in practical reason.'

Against this backdrop, the outcome analysis of the present study becomes critical, as the human capability perspective offers an integrated approach on the role of education as a direct measure of well-being, and freedom as an indirect influence on social change and economic production (Tilak 2002a: 204). Though the review of the literature highlights diverse aspects, the empirical gaps set the conditions for the current work. Although the literature on the capabilities perspective argues about various issues in detail, some of them interchangeably use the human development and capabilities approaches in the analyses. A closer reading of the arguments underlines that the capabilities approach is broader in its conception, which goes beyond the calculus part of human development.[2] Though both are drawn broadly from the perspectives of Mahbub ul Haq (2003) and Sen (1999b), the capabilities approach draws more from Sen's contribution. This was later extended by Nussbaum (2011) as well. The current work, with the perspective of the capabilities approach, attempts to analyse educational functionings of the poor. This is important in the context of Sripuram as the capabilities approach '... is unique in its emphasis on assessing development by how well it expands the capabilities of all people' (Fukuda-Parr 2003).

The Complexities

As the literature review touched upon in this chapter captures the social realities, here is an attempt to understand the complexities to throw some light on the unexplored issues so far. This is significant as '... the issue of how to address and accommodate culturally, historically and socially marginalised communities are complex, and there are no universal answers' (*Economic and Political Weekly* 2003: 4284). First, for Thorat (2007), caste- and untouchability-based exclusion and discrimination are primarily structural in nature and comprehensive, multiple in coverage, and involve the denial of equal opportunities, particularly to excluded groups like the former 'untouchables'. But in the case of tribes (often called Adivasis), he underlines that the exclusion is not systemic or structural, and therefore the process of exclusion is different, although in outcome it is like that of former 'untouchables' in many respects, if not all (ibid.: 12). This underscores social complexities considering the mistaken common sense which most often assumes the SCs and STs as 'homogeneous' marginalised groups in the country. As Paul Devitt, quoted in Chambers (1981: 7), put it: 'It is rare to find a body or institution that adequately represents the poor in a certain community or area. Outsiders and government officials invariably find it more profitable and congenial to converse with local influentials than with the uncommunicative poor.'

Tilak's (2002b: 14) work is also an eye-opener as it highlights three critical and complex issues. His analyses explain that the poor have a disadvantage, whether they are in rural or urban areas, or whether they are boys or girls. To provide evidence for the complex issues, he underlines that '... deprivation in education does not end with enrolment in schools. The poor are more likely to drop out of the system, often relapsing into illiteracy and ignorance' (ibid.: 17). Also, Gang, Sen and Yun (2004: 21) found that '... while there is little difference in the poverty rates between SC and ST households, the causes of the incidence of poverty in these two social groups are not the same'. There '... is a difference in the strength of the poverty-reducing effect of occupation for SC and non-scheduled households that leaves more SC households in poverty' (ibid.: 17). These complexities have, however, not been discussed in detail in the literature. Most often the situation of the SCs and STs is considered similar. Sengupta, Raveendran and Kannan (2008: 52) in their analysis underscore that the poverty trend among Muslims seems to be more disappointing than that among the SC/ST population.[3]

In this context, it is appropriate to mention Thorat (2007: 25), as 'Andhra Pradesh was the only State that had both Human Development Index (HDI) and Human Poverty Index (HPI) lower than the all-India average. This means that it had both low attainment and low deprivation whereas indices for other States indicate a different relationship, where low HDI is matched with high HPI.'

This underscores the limitations of 'generalisability' in the country. It is mainly because of the social complexities in its structural and institutional arrangements. Hence, a deterministic way of explaining social exclusion and deprivation either through indexing the people in numbers or through certainties of the same arguments is not sufficient to understand the social reality.[4]

The Critiques

Among the available literature, Collins's (2005: 10) critique is worth mentioning. In her position against absolutism, she vehemently criticises how poverty is measured in official definitions, usually compiled by 'experts' who themselves are not poor. The knowledge of poor households, she further adds, about the complex negotiation between means and ends, and the stressful impact of a scrutinising social assistance system, have much to teach those who write and speak about poverty but who do not experience it themselves (ibid.: 28). Quoting Max-Neef (1991), Collins writes: '... [A]n income poverty line represents an abstraction from lived experience in which important contextual factors are not considered' (quoted in Collins 2005: 10). This underscores the limitations of 'statistical' finalities of the subjective well-being where the complexities of poverty are often overlooked.

There are necessary caveats one can highlight here. For instance, 'assuming homogeneity can lead to a masking of the differences that exist within communities based on gender, age, ethnicity or some other factor. Assuming harmony can lead to a failure to take into account intra-communal differences' (ibid.: 14). Wankhede (2001) raises the same point in the Indian context:

> ... while analysing their social and cultural background, the scheduled castes in general in the country and in the state, in particular, do not form a monolithic group and have a social hierarchy and practice of untouchability among themselves. Therefore, the issue of treating them as a homogeneous category is still to be questioned seriously. (Ibid.: 1558)

These critiques are significant to the present work in its attempt to compare the marginalised groups with the non-marginalised along the lines of caste and class dynamics in Sripuram. Even though there have been numerous writings against the absolutist approach (Sen 1999b; Tilak 2002a, among others), the central analyses of poverty studies, as mentioned earlier, have, however, been 'dominated' by economic determinism in India: '[T]here is a danger in seeing poverty in the narrow terms of income deprivation, and then justifying investment in education, health care and so forth on the ground that they are a good means to an end of reducing income poverty' (Sen 1999b: 92). In recent times, however, this has 'reluctantly' been admitted: '[T]he high order of continuing exclusion induced deprivation of disadvantaged groups of SCs and STs indicates that addressing social exclusion is often a far more difficult challenge than material poverty' (Thorat 2007: 54).

Thus, economic inequality 'is not the only form of inequality and the distribution of income (or of expenditure) does not always provide the most revealing picture even of economic inequality' (Béteille 2003: 4458). In his critique on Sen, Béteille (1993: 755) adds that 'the strength of Sen's urge to demonstrate the importance of the norm of equality as the basis of a just society leads him to neglect the obvious fact that inequality too is supported by norms'. Considering this, it is pertinent to contextualise the subjective definition:

> It is true that the method suggested is basically a method measuring the extent of malnutrition not attributable to wasteful spending, but I think it would give the fairest index of poverty, particularly if the results gained by its use were correlated with other findings based on standards of over-crowding, household amenities, *education* and so on. (Townsend 1954: 135, emphasis added).

Although it is meaningful to include education, it is also reductionistic when Townsend emphasises the extent of malnutrition. For example, the fast-food culture of the rich and the non-poor could mean that they are malnourished, even though they are not poor. While the mainstream sociological perspective naturally adopts a subjective definition of poverty which is relative in its conception, Béteille raises doubt. To him, 'where the concept of absolute poverty is too narrow and restrictive, that of relative poverty is too vague and subjective' (Béteille 2003: 4462).

Analytical Scope

This analysis illustrates a variety of analytical categories along with various caveats. In turn, it has enlarged the scope for the present research, which engages with the works mentioned in the previous sections with ethnographic reflexivity. In this process, the framework attempts to take up an interdisciplinary perspective of the sociology of education within the paradigm of the capabilities approach in India. It is exploratory in design, as most of the research on education and poverty in the country so far 'has focused on the human capital dimension of education, more specifically education as a means of reducing poverty ...' (Tilak 2002a: 198). This limitation has also been aptly captured as, in India, 'the attempts made in developing concept and methodology to assess the impact of social exclusion on human deprivation are, however, limited in number' (Thorat 2007: 2).

The implication of the capabilities approach on the sociology of education, in Unterhalter's (2003a: 668) assessment, is with '... the ethical concerns with the individual on which both Sen and Nussbaum draw' to 'give a much fuller and more demanding means to evaluate and call for accountability about education than human capital theory'. She further adds: 'It provides a new perspective for addressing distributional issues and concerns with educational equality' (ibid.). Béteille's (2003: 4458) suggestion could be mentioned in this regard. Intellectuals in a democracy, he suggests, 'take pride in being critics of the establishment, and since planning and development are to be the responsibilities of the government, evidence of increasing poverty and inequality received special attention'. However, the review exercise highlights the absence of work in sociology on the capabilities approach in India. This, according to Béteille, could be because 'poverty studies in India have been the preserve of economists rather than sociologists' (ibid.: 4455). Gang, Sen and Yun (2004: 2) too underline that, '[d] espite the existence of large gaps in poverty rates between scheduled and non-scheduled groups, very few studies have specifically and systematically investigated the causes of the disparity'.

The current analyses also points out the gaps in the discourse. One scholar wrote that '... schools have failed to provide adequate academic support to Dalit and Adivasi children, a majority of whom come from non-literate and poorly educated homes' (Nambissan 2000). She further adds that the social discrimination experienced by Dalit and Adivasi children within the portals of the school is scarcely acknowledged by school actors and indeed by researchers. Also, Sengupta, Raveendran and Kannan (2008: 55) analysed that the impact of better education on poverty reduction was not uniform among different social groups. This specification supports the adaptive preferences of the educated underemployed youths (EUEY) and educated unemployed youths (EUY) of the present work, where the differences in functionings as well as capability formations are presented in Sripuram. This gap can be observed in other literature which underscores the same point. To quote: '... the likelihood of being in poverty differs across groups. For example, education may be less effective in reducing the probability of being poor in scheduled households relative to non-scheduled households' (Gang, Sen and Yun 2004: 13). Thus, it is important to note that the abject poor are excluded from adequate access to institutions even at the most local level and that their institutional links are generally thin (Cleaver 2005: 902).

Considering that the key role of education is to be an agent of change, 'it is worth seeing educational achievements among those deprived sections' (Wankhede 2001: 1553). This comes with a caveat of mistaken treatment of the caste system as a similar category. In brief, one can observe that any simple disaggregation of social groups across, for example, education (literacy rate, enrolment ratio), health (child mortality), access to resources (landownership, employment rate), and urbanisation underlines that the SCs and STs lag behind other sections of Indian society (Thorat 2007: 3). Adequate care has to be taken so that '... whether the focus is on pre-primary, primary or post-primary education, there continues to be a need to understand *how* the purported link between education and poverty reduction can be realised in particular contexts' (Rose and Dyer 2006, quoted in King, McGrath and Rose 2007: 351). This is crucial because '... the success and failure of all our programmes and policies including those for promoting economic growth, will have to be reckoned in terms of how they have fulfilled this basic objective of improving the welfare of the common people' (Sengupta, Raveendran and Kannan 2008: 49).

The capabilities perspective, in this context, is necessarily an apt focal point: 'Amartya Şen's ideas provide the core principles of a development approach whose flexible framework allows policy-makers to analyse diverse challenges that poor people and poor countries face, rather than imposing a rigid orthodoxy with a set of policy prescriptions' (Fukuda-Parr 2003: 302). This is considering the recent suggestion of economic limitations where '... both social and economic deprivations are facts of life in India, but the social deprivation arising out of social identity (i.e., caste/community) seems to be so deeply entrenched that it cannot be brushed aside by addressing only economic deprivation' (Sengupta, Raveendran and Kannan 2008: 60). This underscores the importance of crossing the disciplinary boundaries to understand the elusive nature of social reality. The interdisciplinary nature of the capabilities approach thus provides the perspective for intersectional analysis of the social construction of capabilities in Sripuram.

Most of the literature reviewed in this chapter concerns the disadvantaged status of the SCs and STs in almost all spheres including education (Béteille 2003; Nambissan 2000; Tilak 2002b; Wankhede 2001). This historical malady reinforces the poverty trap in the process of capability formations. Hence, the thesis on the social construction of capabilities is significant where the outcome analyses the social dynamics at the intersection of economic deprivation, and social exclusion of the poor gains momentum. In this effort, the current work contrasts the marginalised groups (who have been constitutionally scheduled) with the non-marginalised, from a comparative perspective. Considering the socio-economic mobility of the poor, the intersectional analysis of caste and class in educational outcomes adds a fresh dimension to the understanding of the developmental processes in India.[5]

Notes

1. The Census enumeration and other data collection are done by the officials of the formal bureaucratic structures in India.

2. HDIs are calculated regularly by the United Nations Development Programme (UNDP). Based on this, the Human Development Reports are generated every year with a thematic focus.

3. These complexities in Sripuram have, however, 'naturally' been addressed where there are no ST or Muslim men in the village.

4. This, for instance, primarily considers all the SCs as homogeneously poor and socially excluded. In addition to this perception at the societal level,

mainstream academia, especially education research, is critical of the private players. This is despite the fact that the government is notorious for its poor quality of schooling, which the common people are now rejecting. Against this backdrop, there is an experiential fact that most of the government servants, including academicians, do not send their children to these schools for quality reasons. The gap between the academia's personal 'choice' and professional 'voice' is a paradox in India (Venkataraman 2019).

5. Social mobility is the movement of individuals or groups between different positions in society. Against this backdrop, this research analyses the significance of education on both upward as well as downward mobility.

three

Intersectional Implications of Capabilities Formation*

The central argument of this chapter conceptualises intersections of primordial identities. The concept of intersection underscores how diverse social positions interact in Sripuram. As intersectionality is 'the mutually constitutive relations among social identities' (Shields 2008: 301), the interactions of caste, class and gender in education are conceptualised to delineate the social constructions of capabilities.

As a complex system, intersectionality assumes a methodology that 'sees everything as interactions, not "main effects"' (Choo and Ferree 2010: 136). According to Shields (2008: 306), 'The theoretical compatibility and historic links between intersectionality theory and qualitative methods imply that the method and the theory are always already necessary to one another. Intersectionality theory, by virtue of its description of multi-dimensional nature of identity makes investigation through qualitative seem both natural and necessary.' This chapter highlights the role of in/tangible structural factors in educational outcomes in the village of Sripuram. An intersection-based analysis is crucial—even the acclaimed academic works of Srinivas and Béteille have somewhat overlooked these dimensions.[1] This limitation is not a deliberate avoidance on the scholars' part, as one must acknowledge the emerging interest in intersectional research studies in recent years. Methodologically, intersectionality-specific research has yet to capture mainstream narratives. The literature on the intersections of caste, class and gender in education is especially

*Originally published in *Development in Practice* 25 (8), November 2015: 1170–81.

thin in the case of Tamil Nadu. This is indeed a critical research vacuum, as gender is 'the all-inclusive negative parameter conferring cumulative and competing disadvantages on women' (Chanana 1993: 69). This vacuum can, however, be highlighted in the light of diverse feminist discourse intensely deconstructing various other aspects of our stratified society.[2] Thus, this chapter will underscore how the differential outcomes in both functionings and capabilities are influenced by the intersectionality of caste, class and gender in both education and employment.

Intersectionality: Methodological Implications

Intersectionality in this chapter will involve a methodological deconstruction of the interactions of caste, class and gender in education. The effort is to analyse the social construction of capabilities by examining these diverse factors in Sripuram. These intersections are complicated due to their active role in identity formations. For instance, though caste is being increasingly theorised as a backward division of labour(ers) by mainstream research (Ambedkar 2014; Deliege 2011; Deshpande 2008; Nambissan 2000; Thorat 2007), most of the villagers consider it as their social identity. This is in addition to other intersecting factors in consolidating the 'self', where the role of education is seemingly minimal. This could be due to systemic failures in critically looking at identity formations. The curricular as well as pedagogic arrangements seem to be far away from the everydayness where one can observe the clash of actual and ideal worldviews.

Thus, the everyday negotiations of individuals at the boundaries of diverse identities are gendered with respect to caste and class, and underscore the importance of analysing these beyond the deterministic standpoints. These perspectives often re/produce the same narratives of victimhood in un/critically repeating ideological determinism. The depiction of complex social realities is often simplified in reductionist worldviews by mainstream narratives. It seems this is due to the failure in accounting for 'the multiplicity of social categories' (Dunn 1993: 66) that obscure the intersections of diverse socio-economic realities.

CASTE AND CLASS IN SRIPURAM

The primordial identities of caste and its sociological implications on the class positions of individuals have conceptual importance in the intersectional analysis of India. The class system 'overlaps to a considerable extent with the caste structure, but also cuts across it at a number of points' (Béteille 1965a: 4). As this structural convergence continues, 'there has been considerable modification of the traditional congruent relationships between caste and social class' (Mencher 1970: 210). The result is that the capability formation of human agencies is conditioned by both the intersectional factors in the village as well as the wider socio-economic contexts outside Sripuram. The current forms of caste and class, because of the social changes, must be contrasted with the earlier descriptions of Sripuram. For instance, in contrast to the description in which 'a villager's caste determined his position in the class system and power hierarchy' (Nandy 1966: 729), this has increasingly been subsumed by the educational status of individuals today. As a result, one can observe a growing dissociation of caste and class mainly due to the emerging social changes: 'With the change from a static, traditional social order to a more dynamic one, the economic and political systems gradually detach themselves from caste and acquire a more autonomous character' (D'Souza 1999: 301).

The social class positions in this newer form are often determined by functional outcomes in which the role of education is increasingly instrumental. Also, Driver's (1982: 251) findings point to the 'considerable independence between social class and the caste hierarchy, between caste and several status-groupings, and between social class and some status-groupings'. For him, such independence means that the concept of '"status summation" has quite limited applicability today in South India' (ibid.). As this underlines the importance of intersectionality, it is pertinent to mention Deliege's (2011) analysis:

> The problem of class in rural India has historically been twofold: first, castes have corresponded only very imperfectly to social classes, and second, the analysis of Indian society in terms of classes has been particularly fraught because of the non-recognition of such categories by Indians themselves. However, class analysis may be increasingly useful today. (Ibid.: 52)

Regarding the intersectionality of caste and class, the first noticeable change in Sripuram was that of the working relationship between the OBCs and the Pallars. This runs counter to the caste-based economic interdependence of earlier times when the Pallars, as agricultural labourers (often known as Pannayals), used to work for the Mirasdars. Education-based economic mobility is seemingly the determinant of this change. The Mirasdars, who were predominantly Brahmins in the earlier years, have now almost given up their landholdings. This seems to be due to their increased economic mobility-driven emigration to the cities. The OBC 'neo-elites' have replaced the old order. The result is that the Pallar Pannayal now works under the OBC Mirasdar where one can see the near-absence of Brahmins in agriculture. This marks a changed social reality as 'the correspondence between caste status and class positions has probably diminished over time, where the stratification system has become more open' (Fuller 2012: *xx*). It must be noted that there were only two Brahmin landowners in the village at the time of this study. Neither of them was interested in agriculture. This highlights that 'caste hierarchy and occupational hierarchy are not parallel to one another' (Driver 1982: 228). However, this does not mean that the Brahmins have become economically poor over the years. The life-chances of the Brahmins have been 'expectantly' better than those of the Pallars, even when their economic status are similar in Sripuram. This is mainly due to historical reasons: the 'lower' the caste, greater the chances of being socio-economically poor in the country. Given their socio-economic dispositions, the erstwhile higher castes can secure better life-chances.

In this context, one can also observe the increasing irrelevance of landownership as a central criterion for identifying the poor in the village today. This indicates the need to appreciate newer forms of social stratification. These newer forms can be understood mainly in terms of the intersectionality of caste, class, gender, education and the employment status of individuals. Caste-based class determinism of social science analysis can, therefore, be revised by giving importance to other relevant forms of analysis. Also, the current ethnographic fieldwork has observed the intersectional aspects within the family structure in Sripuram. It found that the relative deprivation of individuals within the family structure was not the same as that of its class position in the village. The disadvantage is perceivable across age, gender and disability aspects. However, the numerical enumeration of the poor often overlooks the intersectional dynamics (see Tilak 2002a).

Considering this changing economic sphere, the pattern of living as a similar social unit based on caste lines has also begun to shift in Sripuram. This can be contrasted with Béteille's (1965a: 43) description in which 'people belonging to the same group of castes live together, but not necessarily people belonging to the same class'. Today, one can, however, see a newer pattern of living in the Agraharam. In this Brahmin-dominated neighbourhood, there has been a replacement of inhabitation vis-à-vis caste–class intersections. The economic opportunities outside the village have lured the Brahmins to emigrate. This tendency is higher among this group because of their socio-economic capital. Local Brahmins sell their houses in the Agraharam and other properties in the village in favour of an urban life. In light of the neighbourhood's reputation, locals from various other castes compete to buy these properties. Thus, there is an influx of OBCs from outside the village. An interesting sociological fact is that the local Brahmins, though critical of other castes in the village, are seemingly not averse to the influx of other castes from outside. This influx often happens due to class factors; the new house-owners who are all OBCs from outside the village are economically influential enough to counter the Brahmins' exclusivist narratives. As this is a recent development in the neighbourhood, most of them are 'adjusting' to their new lifestyles. The Brahmins, though 'silently' critical of these new entrants, seemingly understand the changing realities in the Agraharam. This is determined by the intersections of diverse factors, as the economics of both the emigrating Brahmins and the immigrating OBCs play a role in the reordering of social class. This is in addition to political developments where demographics often play differential roles. The local Brahmins 'carefully' read the policy narratives of these outcomes. Although this noticeable shift has been partly due to the emigration of the Brahmins, one can trace the influences of the broader politico-economic forces from the 'outside'. Increasing economic necessities have rearranged livelihoods. It can be argued that neither class nor caste may exclusively constitute a community in the future. It is the intersection of diverse societal factors that could play a definite role in the village.

Gender in Intersection

In Sripuram, the interrelations between caste, class and gender in education have brought about significant changes in the social system. These interrelations are exclusive in their nature and form. The notion of exclusiveness should be observed keeping in mind the primordial identities. For instance, aspects of caste endogamy must be mentioned. Marital alliances are generally determined according to similarities of caste and class where decisions are often made within the patriarchal family structure. This can be contrasted against the general view that caste, irrespective of class position, is crucial for conjugal relations.

Thus, the role of patriarchy in both education and employment has its complexities in the social construction of capabilities. For instance, while there is a strikingly significant unevenness in the distribution of education across caste groups (see Paranjape 2007), the social structure places women at a disadvantage even within those inequalities. This unevenness can further be observed in terms of disparities between different layers of education in terms of the intersections of caste and gender.

This unevenness is determined by 'education poverty' (Tilak 2002a), which ensures neither basic capabilities nor functionings in the village.[3] These complexities require an intersectional taxonomy of both structural as well as systemic conditions for human flourishing. The role of the state in addressing these intersections has, however, been politically driven by electoral motives. Subsequently, human agencies are often left with personal responsibilities. This seems to be the result of changing macro-economic structures in line with neo-liberal democracy in India.

In addition, the complexities need to be conceptualised along gendered social realities, where the impact of un/underemployment 'on the intra-household power relationship' (Balasubramanian, Tamizoli and Murugakani 2002) is adverse in nature. In a patriarchal social structure like that of Sripuram, these adversarial 'cooperative conflicts' of the household often limit opportunities for capabilities formations of women. Social institutions influence these structural constraints. Gendered experiences further limit the socio-economic mobility of women in a patriarchal order. It is pertinent to discuss Mala's case in this context who is an educated underemployed Pallar woman.

> L. N. VENKATARAMAN (henceforth Laksh): If you get a job in bigger cities like Madras, will you be able to go considering the paternalist concerns of your family?
> MALA: It is difficult.
> LAKSH: So, may I ask you whether the pressure is because you are a woman? Alternatively, even the men must face the same pressure?
> MALA: Hmm ... the pressure is only for the girls. The family will not allow me to go mainly because I am a girl. They may encourage the boys, but girls are often prevented from venturing out. For the girls, the family thinks for them. (Interview from the field, dated 11 August 2011.)

Mala's experiential reality depicts the constraints where she must adapt her preferences according to her family's wishes. These constraints are often in/directly shaped by other intersections of caste, class and gender in the village. This is seemingly dissimilar to men in the patriarchal social order. Consequently, her educational credentials do not play an instrumental role in subverting the structural constraints. Her adaptive preferences (Teschl and Comim 2005) highlight the self-subordinating realities to thrive inside the structures for apparent reasons of membership. It is indeed surprising how most of the youth including Mala do not question the inequalities determined by socio-economic structures. Though the 'credential education' regime keeps them aware of the developments happening outside due to the proliferation of the mass media, they are generally not critical of their life-worlds.[4] This is similar to the notions of 'we can think, but we cannot do' (see Sweeney and Naish 2001). Accordingly, the uncritical nature of the education credentials complicates the basic capabilities. However, these structural constraints do not necessarily block just the erstwhile lower caste women; in Sripuram, a Brahmin girl's intention to seek employment also needs patriarchal 'approval'. For instance, in Jayanthi's words:

> My elder brother does not want me to work. He said to me, "The family's finances are not going to depend on your work, which require you to roam outside home." But I told him about my interests, that I do not want to waste my education, as I wish to earn at least for a year. (Interview from the field, dated 6 September 2011.)[5]

Thus, primordial hegemonies of caste with the gendered realities of human lives interact with social class factors. Systemic issues further intersect with these structural interactions. For instance, aspects of education including access and outcome are often influenced by these intersections. This is similar to the finding of Dunn (1993) where women have far limited access to both educational and employment resources than men. Against this backdrop, the educated unemployed as well as underemployed youth in Sripuram adequately highlight the complexities of capabilities deprivation.

On a broader level, in this social dynamic, the state has been 'supportive' of the erstwhile lower castes for political and electoral reasons. The notion of a vote bank is a sociological concept coined by Srinivas in 1995 to define the political class's strategies of treating primordial identities such as caste and religious factors as a 'fixed deposit' with which to win elections in India. Furthermore, this must be understood in light of the predominant population base of the non-Brahmins, on whom the political class depends for its electoral survival in Tamil Nadu. For instance, according to the 2011 demographic figures, nearly 70 per cent of the total population in Tamil Nadu were the OBCs (Government of India 2011: 253). In light of this demographic reality in which roughly 93 per cent of the total population is non-Brahmin (which includes both OBCs and SCs), one can find broader policy decisions of a populist nature. This explains why the Brahmins have moved to the greener economic pastures of nearby towns, a result also of the absence of economic opportunities and infrastructure in Sripuram that is typical of any village in the country.

The Dominant Castes who have had direct socio-economic relationships with the local Brahmins are increasingly emulating the latter in their economic planning, and education is one of the first domains they follow. The broader political economy often seems to influence the changing nature and forms of caste in the village. This is explicitly visible due to two essential policy steps: the anti-untouchability laws and the reservation policy in the country. The reservation policy in India is often contrasted in line with the affirmative action policies of the United States (see, for instance, Weisskopf 2004). However, it must be noted that there is a remarkable difference in discrimination along caste lines and racial exclusion experienced in India and the US, respectively. Racial discrimination is most often based on physical appearance such as skin colour. Caste discrimination is inclusive of physical as well as social status. According to sociological literature, individuals are often discriminated against, even when they are economically well-off, if they happen to be from the lower castes. As the accidents of birth determine mobility between castes, exclusion remains a static social factor. Against this backdrop, the Indian state reserves a certain percentage of seats in both education and employment for the erstwhile lower castes and tribes as its own version of an affirmative action policy. While these policy steps are predominantly in support of the erstwhile lower castes, there is unrest as well as livelihood desperation among both orthodox Brahmins and the OBCs in the village. Their perceived marginality due to positive discrimination policies in both education and employment often makes them conscious of their caste identity as well as renders them 'competitive' in both fields. This competitiveness can be seen in their approach to education. It is most often based on instrumental ideals for occupational outcome and economic mobility. At conceptual levels, this confirms the ascent of the human capital notion in education. The 'competitiveness' under this notion is thus complicated because of intermeshing class factors. As class is not only an economic, but also a social category, these complications are often reinforced by education. Thus, the presumed priority of caste as a micro-determinant of social contexts suggests how it can be seen working together with class and education in drawing the boundaries that re/produce complex inequalities. In this intersectional social process, there is an urgent need to conceptualise capitals and capabilities.

Notes

1. This has been acknowledged by Béteille in personal interviews with the author. In his view, gender is an important dimension that 'slipped out' of the central focus in his works (personal interview, dated 6 May 2011).
2. Although this is an inheritance-based division of labour, one can find a complicated picture of variations across regions in the country.
3. The differential outcomes in both capabilities and functioning formations are thus strongly influenced by the intersectionality of caste, class and education in employment in Sripuram.

4. Life-world is an esoteric expression that denotes more or less the 'background' environment of competences, practices and attitudes representable in terms of one's cognitive horizons.

5. Both Mala and Jayanthi are educated underemployed women. However, they represent the two extreme ends of the caste spectrum. While Mala belongs to the Pallar caste, Jayanthi is Brahmin.

four

Education Quality, Employability and Capabilities*

Despite the state government's claims of growth in education in Tamil Nadu (Government of Tamil Nadu 2003: 10), there has been a decrease in enrolment rates in the government schools over the years (Government of India 2008–09: 112). In Sripuram, even the poor are increasingly emigrating out of fee-free government schooling for quality reasons. There are two main factors. One is the erosion of the image of the state, at least in school education, and two, the establishment of private schooling in Tamil Nadu. Though these education 'shops' work mostly for commercial interests, they are popular among the public. This is reflected in the fact that the villagers in Sripuram opt to enroll their children in private schools outside Sripuram, despite the presence of local schools. Students at the local school are mostly orphans.[1] The common perception in the village seems to be that only those who cannot afford private schools enroll in the local school, which, only a few decades previously, had been 'celebrated as a site of secular values in modernising the village'.[2]

Educational Outcome in Sripuram

The analysis of caste-wise enrolment is pertinent, as it will give us a picture of the educational outcomes in the local school (see, for instance, De, Endow and Ghosh 2010; Thorat 2010; Young 2009, among others). Regarding outcome analysis, enrolment by caste-wise categorisation depicts the educational patterns of social groups in the

---

*Originally published in *ASIEN: The German Journal on Contemporary Asia* 127, April 2013: S30–47.

village. In this context, a cursory analysis of the enrolment figures from 1990 to 2018 has underlined a sharp decline of enrolment from the Agraharam (Table 4.1). This trend is being increasingly emulated by the OBCs, who are also moving away from the government school.[3]

TABLE 4.1 Enrolment (Caste-wise Figures) in the Local School in Sripuram, 1990–2018*

Year	*Brahmin*		*OBCs*** *[Non-Brahmin]*		*SCs*		*Total*		*Total*
	Girls	*Boys*	*Girls*	*Boys*	*Girls*	*Boys*	*Girls*	*Boys*	
1990	11	18	146	515	81	131	238	664	902
1991	11	11	147	374	100	123	258	508	766
1992	10	10	172	383	109	127	291	520	811
1993	3	7	185	386	94	133	282	526	808
1994	8	10	159	392	92	148	259	550	809
1995	6	8	174	445	90	145	270	598	868
1996	6	7	200	430	99	150	305	594	899
1997	5	4	221	396	99	122	325	522	847
1998	5	4	208	264	102	118	325	522	847
1999	6	3	219	268	99	110	315	386	701
2000	6	5	206	250	102	129	324	381	705
2001	7	5	214	237	97	123	318	384	702
2002	5	4	209	223	94	126	308	453	761
2003	5	4	208	224	80	98	283	326	609
2004	4	4	182	214	76	89	263	307	570
2005	6	2	186	208	70	80	262	290	552
2006	5	4	177	201	65	70	247	275	522
2007	6	2	182	203	69	68	257	273	530
2008	8	2	167	192	66	77	241	271	512
2009	1	2	146	181	79	85	226	268	494
2010	1	6	141	185	77	81	219	272	491
2011	0	4	127	157	58	57	185	218	403
2012	0	5	121	138	48	58	169	196	365
2013	0	3	96	107	52	59	148	169	317
2014	2	0	63	56	38	25	103	81	184

(contd)

Table 4.1 (contd)

Year	*Brahmin*		*OBCs** [Non-Brahmin]*		*SCs*		*Total*		*Total*
	Girls	*Boys*	*Girls*	*Boys*	*Girls*	*Boys*	*Girls*	*Boys*	
2015	2	0	74	65	43	44	119	109	228
2016	1	0	79	61	31	38	111	99	210
2017	1	0	87	59	36	40	124	99	223
2018	1	0	88	49	33	35	122	84	206

Note: *These enrolment figures can also be considered completion rates due to the 'all-pass' policy of the government. This has been the practice since 2002 in the village school.

**This includes both BCs and MBCs in the village.

Source: Caste-wise enrolment from the school records in Sripuram, 1990–2018.

Though the enrolment figures from among the SCs are relatively constant compared to other social groups, they too follow the trend seen among their upper and middle caste peers: for example, Pallar households are now increasingly sending their children to private schools in Meenakshipuram. This differential approach to education due to the intersecting social factors of caste and class often creates a newer social layer even among the erstwhile lower castes in the village. For this reason, one can observe a small degree of socio-economic distance of educated households like that of the 33-year-old educated underemployed youth Iyappan from the Pallar caste in Keezhatheru today.[4] Iyappan, it must be noted, represents the economically well-off households of the Keezhatheru. His career aspirations through education are similar to those of the other power-elites in the village.

In addition to this, the author's unannounced field visits to both the local school and the orphanage provide a picture of the quality of education in Sripuram. An assessment of basic literacy and numeracy skills of the children reveals a lack of quality. This assessment of quality was based on simple tests conducted by the author on (i) reading and comprehension; (ii) writing from dictation; and (iii) numeracy skills. Though this assessment was conducted at regular intervals during the fieldwork, most of the children were unsuccessful at these tests, with a few exceptions. This is symbolic of the systemic issues in education in Sripuram. However, these issues are often overlooked by teaching 'officials', many of whom, as the author observed during fieldwork, leave school immediately after office hours, even though some of them may have come in late in the morning.

Furthermore, the state's 'generous' all-pass policy promotes children to the next level even without them having learnt anything 'meaningful'. For instance, Ganapathy, a teacher from the local school, when asked what he thought of this policy, and whether it was useful to the students, opined:

> In my opinion, the government's policy of all-pass is a foolish decision ... Students should not stop their education mid-way. If we fail, the student will stop. That is the reason why the government brought in the all-pass scheme ... But the scheme destructs the brilliant student. Even the bright student is carried away by it, and their standard is going down ... Students come with the mindset that they will "pass" even before appearing for the exam ... so there is no interest in learning ... There is no creativity among the students. There is no aim to get the first mark as they know that they will certainly pass, whatever may be the case. (Interview from the field, dated 3 July 2012.)

Some of the teaching staff have accepted the lowering quality standards and cite their inability to discipline children in their informal interactions, due to various factors, for example, government regulations preventing punishments in the school. In this context, another teacher complained: 'On the one hand, the government expects us to provide quality teaching. However, on the other hand, they tie our hands [with newer regulations] only to hold a chalk-piece' (interview from the field, dated 5 July 2012). The headmaster too is supposedly expected to be subservient to hierarchies of the educational bureaucracy in the state. Any innovation, even for improving the outcomes of education, is often discouraged as a 'deviance' from the bureaucratic frameworks (see Drèze and Kingdon 1999).

Against this background, the assessment failures of the eighth standard are more worrisome, as students at this level are relatively older than the others in the school. It seems that the gaps in their education, mainly in literacy and numeracy skills, are setting the stage for inferior capability formations. This has often been cited as a challenge by the educated un/underemployed youths. Most of the youths have said that the students of Sripuram often perform poorly in Meenakshipuram.[5] For instance, Mala, a 24-year-old Pallar woman with a Bachelor's degree in History, compares the local school with Satsangh School in Meenakshipuram:

> I started realising what education is only after going to Satsangh School in Meenakshipuram. I started getting interested in studying out there ... Schools outside will normally fail you for one year if you are coming from the local Sripuram school ... Because we never get anything out of the local school. So after joining there for ninth, merely thinking about the tenth board exam was too scary. (Interview from the field, dated 11 August 2011.)

Thus, the dual developmental deficits, both regarding functionings and capabilities, must be analysed from the intersectional social facts. As class as well as caste factors mostly determine the system of education, the extreme difference in quality often perpetuates the mainstream social order. As a microscopic reality, Sripuram reflects the educational status of Tamil Nadu. For all the expected systemic reasons, it seems that the notion of quality exists only in the official reports, which, despite the endless number of figures and facts it contains, does not reflect the everyday complexities of the local school.

Education Quality and Employability in Sripuram

In modern times, the reasons of un/underemployment are mostly related to issues of education quality in any country. India is no different. '[E]ducation is one of the toughest problems that Man is called upon to handle. The effort must however be made because, in the last analysis, it is education alone that stands between Man and Catastrophe' (Naik 1979: 185). Developmental demands of our post-colonial society have seemingly been met by 'certified' knowledge. As functional literacy becomes the passport for any salaried employment, one needs to highlight the importance of quality. Quality in education is primarily determined by the stakeholders; it is affected by parental negligence due to socio-economic deprivation (involuntary) and bureaucratic apathy (voluntary).

Though quality is an important determinant of employability, the system most often fails the poor. As the state-owned schools in the country are known for their poor quality outcomes in education (see, for instance, Kumar 2004; Kumar and Sarangapani 2004; Valeskar 2010, among others), the attributes of employability of the poor fail even in the initial years of education itself. In this context, it is pertinent to mention Iyappan from Sripuram, whom we came across earlier. Iyappan has many educational qualifications, which include a Bachelors in Commerce (B.Com), Bachelors in Physical Education (B.PEd), Diploma in Computer Application (DCA), Diploma in Cooperative Management (D.Coop), Jewel Appraisal and Postgraduate Diploma in Yoga. As an educated youth from the Pallar caste, his employment status has changed during different phases of this fieldwork. This is mainly due to the volatility of employment in the region. He sometimes works in the informal economies of Meenakshipuram, or passes his time helping others in order to further his political aspirations.[6] The author asked Iyappan about the quality of education and its relevance for employability today:

> LAKSH: As you have studied in so many different institutions, may I ask you of their role in your career? ... What is their role in getting salaried employment? Is there any use of these institutions?
>
> IYAPPAN: Nothing. Whatever we get is only with our skills and smartness.
>
> LAKSH: So can we say that you went to all these institutions just to get the degree certificates?
>
> IYAPPAN: Not really. However, the schools are useless. Our success depends only on our effort. If one studies well, he can have a good life ahead. (Interview from the field, dated 23 September 2012.)

It must be mentioned that Iyappan's critical reflections on the school education system, as an EUEY in the village, are important. His experiential opinion as a Pallar youth, furthermore, strengthens the case of education, which is deplorable. In addition to this, state institutions still enjoy a 'good' public image for their quality in higher education. Because of this, one can see a reverse immigration of the non-poor in government higher education institutions, where the poor and the deprived often fail to gain entry due to heavy competition. The poor have to be content with the alternatives available to them because of their inability to enter fee-charging private schools as well as their exclusion from quality higher institutions in the name of merit and fee-barriers. These adaptive preferences can be conceptualised in line with Sen's (1999b: 87–110) notion of the poor's complicity in perpetuating their deprivation. Their un/underemployability must also be understood with respect to their employers' expectations, which are high due to a 'culture of competitive aggressiveness' (Kumar 2004: 21). The economically poor like Selvam (a 22-year old OBC male with a Bachelor's degree in Business Administration working as a casual labourer in Meenakshipuram) and others, for instance, go to private colleges in Tanjore, even though those are notorious for their quality standards. The rationale behind this choice is seemingly to 'stand in the queue' for salaried employment at least with a certificate in hand. Thus, employability becomes the crucial factor for functional outcomes in education.[7] This must be seen considering the heightened market-capitalism in the country. Though approaching education merely for employment limits the concept of functionings, it is one of the leads for broader capability formations at present. The notion of capability, as individuals' ability to take independent decisions, in addition to acquiring the necessary life-skills, for instance, is mostly determined by their earning abilities. Due to this, the functional outcome becomes a critical developmental factor in the functionings analysis of the capabilities approach. It is pertinent to mention Iyappan's views again:

> LAKSH: As you are 'working hard' even to get [this temporary] job with lots of degrees and diplomas, what are the usual hurdles you face in your effort to get a salaried job?
> IYAPPAN: The hurdles are mainly due to a large number of educated people vying for the limited jobs available. Also, there is a high level of competition. Whoever is ready to bribe more will get the best bid. This is the situation in Tamil Nadu today.
> LAKSH: Is this for salaried employment in the government?
> IYAPPAN: Yes it is ... No one appoints us merely because we have suitable qualifications for the available job. The amount we bribe will mostly determine it. (Interview from the field, dated 23 September 2012.)

Also, quality in education in the context of Sripuram can be seen in the progressive changes in students' knowledge, behaviour, attitudes and values. These intangible aspects are important for functional outcomes, and have a central role in capabilities formations. This sets the background for the necessity of approaching quality in education when we consider employability. However, it must be reiterated that though there is a conceptual limitation to looking at the education quality in relation to employability, the current analysis attempts to understand broader implications beyond the instrumentalism. Thus, the analysis is inclusive of ideals of both human capital as well as the capabilities approach in education.

The present research considers employability as an aspect of quality in education, as this includes its usefulness for people's work and careers. This has been conceptualised by the author mainly through his regular interactions with the educated un/underemployed youths in Sripuram. The case of Iyappan mentioned earlier aptly highlights the decaying condition of public institutions in terms of quality services, and the dysfunctional entry barriers. The consequence is that the poor are often left with the secondary institutions, while the non-poor opt differently. Against this background, the local school, though managed by a Brahmin family over the years, is not perceived as 'their' school by the Agraharam. This is in sharp contrast to the past where the school catered mainly to Brahmin children. The employment-centric 'quality' pressures from the macro-economy push the non-poor (who are mostly the Brahmins in Sripuram) to private English-medium schools in Meenakshipuram. The enrolment figures mentioned in Table 4.1 must be seen in this context. The everyday visits of the author to the local school revealed that the inferior nature of education quality was due to various systemic factors. This includes issues with training, policy confusions due to change of political regimes, and endless other systemic factors. This neither ensures the opportunities for capabilities formations nor provides any basic skills. It is challenging to find a handful of individuals who have been successful in obtaining salaried employment. This institutional failure can be seen in both the local school as well as the orphanage in the village.[8]

This systemic mismatch between education and employment most often provides lesser life-chances to the poor. Even though this can also be due to weak social capital, the essential point to be highlighted is the role of education in re/producing the social hierarchy in Sripuram. For instance, it was rare to find a well-placed individual among the Pallars who had graduated from the local school since its inception in 1925. Although this would be difficult today even among the

Brahmins, given their move away from the government school for reasons described earlier, it is the differential outcome across diverse social groups in the village that is of consequence here. It would seem that an individual's un/employability in the formal labour market is mainly due to the inferior quality of the education that they have received over the years. The predominant reason, at least from the local school's perspective, is the over-bureaucratised education system and its failures to match labour market expectations. For instance, the only teacher who enrolled his now-grown daughter in the local school for ideological reasons regretted his decision, according to his telephonic talk with the author, dated 25 September 2013. He was disappointed in his daughter's interpretative skills and spoken English. This basic training, in his opinion, was not available at the government school where his daughter was 'forced' to study due to his 'ideal faith' in the government system, in which he thrives as a teacher. His daughter, with an engineering degree, reportedly failed to get recruited in the campus interviews.

Thus, the inferior quality of the 'fee-free' government school most often adds the burden of unemployment to the poor people's future. This burden is doubled in the case of the girl child. In a patriarchal order, a girl living in a village is often pushed to the social margins. For example, Karuppaiah is an economically poor Vellalar (non-Brahmin/OBC) man in Sripuram. He has six daughters, all of them 'highly' qualified (with M.Com, M.Phil, etc., degrees). They work in the informal economies, which also includes the unrecognised private schools, in Meenakshipuram. The economic necessity of the family drives these women to survive in the informal economies where they fail to get 'decent' employment at par with their qualifications; they become a 'negative' reference for the poor to justify the futility of education in the neighbourhood. Also, it must be noted that none of Karuppaiah's daughters is married. This is important in the context of an Indian village where marriage is considered a natural progression in life, and as a collectivist social order, individuals are often ridiculed for any deviance from the normative societal expectations.

This failure to gain education-appropriate employment confirms that 'the children are strongly affected by the human capital possessed by their parents' (Coleman 1988: S110). These young women's educational success has neither ensured them the broader notions of capabilities nor the skill to compete in the employment market. Generally, the OBCs view this as a systemic failure of the poor. In contrast, the Brahmins view the same as an agentic failure to acquire quality education. This is true if we contrast the case of Karuppaiah's daughters with that of Iyyappan, the Dalit youth who has multiple degrees. His status of being un/underemployed is not visible due to his continuous socio-political engagements in the village; his case holds the 'grain of truth', where individuals often accumulate degrees without 'real' freedom. (Jeffrey, Jeffery and Jeffery 2010). The poor often fail due to entry barriers when it comes to 'cultural capital' and the hegemonic meritocratic demands.

In addition to this, interestingly, individuals (with exceptions like Iyappan) generally do not complain about the role of institutions in their failure in getting secure employment. They usually hold themselves responsible, instead of blaming 'others'. Only when the author probed specifically about the role of the quality of education in their inability to get salaried employment did the educated un/underemployed youths provide a critical picture of it. This may be due to their inability to perceive the importance of how socio-economic forces influence their lives. It may also be because of the neo-liberal socio-economic reality, where failures are most often considered 'individual cases' by the state.

The employment-centric notions of education within the neo-liberal set-up have also forced the Pallars to be part of the human capital approach (HCA) ideals. Shrinking employment avenues in the village and the changing nature of the political economy often facilitate this reinforcement in Sripuram. The result is increasing enrolment in private schools even by the poor for quality reasons. This aspect has, however, been analysed in mainstream literature generally in terms of systemic comparisons.[9] In light of these intersectional education facts, one can presume that there is an active interaction between rising unemployment and the inferior educational provisioning of the government. Mainstream employment research must conceptualise this aspect.

The trend of underemployment, like that faced by Selvam and others in Sripuram, is a form of hidden unemployment. The systemic failures due to quality make the underemployed youths 'misfits' while securing economic livelihood. This is because employability is generally determined by the labour market where the definition of quality is based on the ideals of HCA. The result is that the poor continuously engage in the rate-of-returns and cost–benefit analyses of education in everyday lives. This forbids them from benefitting from the central tenets of the capabilities approach. Thus, neither do individual agencies treat education with the broader notions of capabilities, nor does their employment-centric approach assure them of jobs. The primary reason for this dichotomy is a systemic one.

Education Quality and Capabilities

The present research understands capabilities as the accumulation of a diverse set of functionings in the lives of individuals. For this, the central arguments have been collected from the observations of both orphan children[10] and the educated un/underemployed youths in Sripuram. As these groups have been conceived fundamentally as poor in the study, it is pertinent to mention the importance of the quality of education in capabilities formations. The process of children becoming adults is mostly shaped by the educational institutions they are part of; any shortcoming in quality is at the cost of capabilities formations. This is due to intrinsic links between the evaluative spaces of both functionings and capabilities.

The education system in Tamil Nadu is similar to that of other states in India, which have generally been unsuccessful in converting natural abilities into capabilities. Philosophically, education is expected to shape an individual's choices and preferences for growth and development. As the capabilities approach '... honours individual choices and seeks to avoid authoritarian outcomes' (Jackson 2005: 103), the education system seemingly fails to identify agentic potentialities in Tamil Nadu. The multitude of institutions that have come up in the state fail to provide direction for the broader aspects of capabilities and functionings formations. The state system, for instance, is most often unsuccessful in school education. Inferior quality has been systemically ensured by programme-specific bureaucracy and lethargic parents. The sufferers are naturally the children who often do not know the broader educational implications this may have on their future. In the context of Sripuram, although it is essential that reading habits be cultivated among the students, neither does the local school does have a library, nor does it have any plan to establish one in the days to come. The school administration, however, showed the author an old cupboard of dusty books as the 'library'. For official requirements, the authorities even maintain a register with 'live' entries. This highlights the fact that an important avenue of functionings as well as conversion factors for capability formations is visibly weak in the village.[11] These weak links are seen in the everyday lives of both the orphan children, and the EUEYs and EUYs who are waiting to, respectively, enhance their learning and secure salaried employment through education.

This raises an important question. Are the needy individuals powerful enough to exercise their educational functionings for their capabilities? Answering this question in the neo-liberal state requires complex analyses. India's political economy has been carefully withdrawing from social commitments. The poor children, irrespective of their caste affiliations, do not have options other than to stay in government schools. Social re/production at a broader level stabilises the status quo in favour of the non-poor. The non-poor, who are mostly from the erstwhile higher castes in Sripuram, can send their children to paid private schools in Meenakshipuram which adapt themselves to the demands of the labour market. For instance, guided by the boom in information technology (IT) in Tamil Nadu, computer education is now taught in all private schools. The local school, by contrast, is 'bombarded' with an array of governmental guidelines, which often instantly change with changing political regimes. The result is the systemic re/production of misfits where functional illiteracy is the reality.

Additionally, in Tamil Nadu, admission to government teacher-training institutes requires a high percentage of marks, as those passing out of them are assured jobs available in the public services. Hence, only the meritorious students (who have obtained good marks in school) can get trained in these institutes. However, it is surprising how these 'quality' students are becoming under-performing teachers. Though these teachers earn phenomenally high salaries and other benefits compared to their colleagues in private schools, most of them do not provide quality teaching. This is seemingly due to the pervading systemic laxity on account of the security of the tenure of a 'government servant' or the legal protection they enjoy to retain service until retirement. The poor and the marginalised become the worst sufferers of this vicious cycle of inferior schooling. This, to a large extent, does not ensure better life-chances or, what the development literature calls the conversion factors for both functionings as well as capabilities formations.

As the ability to realise one's capability is decided by education, it is important to conceptualise it keeping in mind the social structure and individual agencies. The villagers of Sripuram can be seen making independent decisions regarding taking up a career, instead of following the ascriptive caste-based division of labour; engaging in caste exogamy; emigrating out of the village against other preferences and assertive reasoning, etc. The main point is whether or not these aspects are functional, and if they have the potential for capabilities formations due to an individual's choices and preferences.

Capabilities formation is mainly conditioned by intersectional dynamics in the village. Here, one can observe the influences of the broader socio-economic contexts of the state. For instance, the political economy of Tamil Nadu revolves mainly around the demographic where nearly 94 per cent of the population is non-Brahmin.[12] Policy decision-making at the macro-level has been accommodating the interests of 'non-Brahmins' in the name of social welfare. This has been the rationale for trying to correct historical injustices done over the years to the erstwhile lower castes. The central argument against this is the perceived fear of 'others': the erstwhile higher castes (Brahmins, in the case of Sripuram) are seemingly afraid of a shrinkage in the potential welfare benefits they might enjoy in state policies. A reservation of 69 per cent for non-Brahmins with the remaining 31 per cent open to all, including the meritorious 'others', has convinced the Brahmins to approach education with an occupational outcome. This is a break from the past when they have historically been known for approaching education for knowledge's sake.

Though education is itself a capability, the broader notions of functionings formation and employment choices are available only with higher levels of knowledge. Hence, higher education is becoming a critical factor for capabilities formations. The nature of capabilities formation, against this backdrop, is mainly determined by the opportunity-sets available in the village. This has, however, not been explicitly discussed in mainstream literature, where it has been analysed generally with regard to human capital notions. This limits capability-specific analysis in India.

By contrast, the central arguments of this chapter have highlighted that the intersectional social factors are influential in both functionings and capabilities formations. Though the development literature underlines that 'both capabilities and functionings are, to a large extent, determined culturally' (Jackson 2005: 117), this has been an under-researched subject in India so far. The functionings failures must then be contrasted against the perception that Tamil Nadu is one of the developed regions in the country. The failures in the evaluative spaces of the capabilities approach question this, considering the notions of Drèze and Sen (1999: 10, in *India: Economic Development and Social Opportunity*): 'One way of seeing development is regarding the expansion of the real freedoms that the citizens enjoy to pursue the objectives they have reason to value, and in this sense, the expansion of human capability can be, broadly, seen as the central feature of the process of development.'

Notes

1. It must be noted that the orphanage in Sripuram caters to the educational needs of children from broken families in the surrounding villages in Tanjore district.

2. Notes from Béteille's personal communication with the author, dated 6 May 2011.

3. The emigrations of villagers from the local school are mostly involuntary due to the perceived quality predicaments of the state system at present. This is similar to the status of government schools across the country.

4. Keezhatheru is the street in Sripuram where the SCs live. This street has other names such as Vadakkutheru (North Street). It is to be mentioned that Béteille (1965a: 25–26) discussed Keezhatheru in the nomenclature of Palla Cheri. The tag of *cheri* (meaning 'slum' in Tamil) has disappeared from everyday usage, with only a few of the village elders remembering this term. As discussed earlier, though the exclusivist residential unit of other castes (of both Brahmins and OBCs) is changing, Keezhatheru is still the exclusive residential unit of the Pallars. These subtle changes have mostly been due to various socio-economic factors over the years.

5. It must be mentioned that Sripuram residents had to send their children to Meenakshipuram after the eighth standard at the time of this study. The

situation was the same during the period of Béteille's fieldwork in 1959–60 as well (personal interview, dated 6 May 2011).

6. During the fieldwork in April 2012, Iyappan was working as a contract teacher for Physical Education in a nearby government school. Though it was a temporary job under the Sarva Shiksha Abhiyan (SSA), he told the author about the financial burdens he had to take on in the form of a bribe to get this short-term assignment. He hopes to get a permanent position there by 'working hard'. SSA is a centrally sponsored scheme in line with the global goals of Education for All (EFA) in India.

7. For further discussion on employability, see, for instance, Hinchliffe and Jolly (2011); Støren and Aamodt (2010); Tomlinson (2008); Venkataraman (2013), among others.

8. The only caveat is that we can still find a few 'successful' Brahmin youths who were from the local school in Sripuram. However, their success could mostly be due to the historicity of their (knowledge-centric) background. Also, one must be aware of the decrease of Brahmin enrolment in the government school (Table 4.1).

9. Though the literature has been successful in focusing on quality, one can still find a vacuum in sociological insights in education research in India. See, for instance, Bajpai and Goyal (2004); Dyer (1996a); Kumar (2004, 2005, 2007); Kumar and Sarangapani (2004); Naik (1979); Rampal (2004); Velaskar (2010), among others. Analysing employability and capability, against this backdrop, is once again an under-researched area in Indian education.

10. The term 'orphan' in this study is used to describe children who have lost either one or both parents. In addition, they come from a background of familial poverty, which pushes the children to the orphanage.

11. According to the capabilities literature, conversion factors represent how many functionings one can get out of a good or service.

12. According to the latest Census figures, this includes nearly 70 per cent OBCs (Government of India 2011).

five

Poverty and Education in Sripuram*

The Poor: Definition and Identification

Poverty 'persists even in countries that are economically advanced and have little population growth, and this has led sociologists to be sceptical about the assumption of a simple relationship between poverty, inequality and economic backwardness' (Béteille 2003: 4457). Poverty in Tamil Nadu, one of the high-growth regions of India, reflects this. Social classes in Sripuram can be re/produced in the lifestyles of the individuals. Class positions can be understood through an individual's place in the occupational structure of the village. Even though individual consumption patterns often signal social class, the relative deprivations of the different members of the same family, for instance, might not be the same, despite them belonging to the same class positions, but vary with age, gender and aspects of dis/ability.[1] However, the numerical enumeration of the poor often overlooks the intersectional dynamics around them. Class analyses are often non-sociological: 'The majority of the studies of poverty using head-count measures have taken the individual or household as the unit. The "classes" with which these studies deal are statistical rather than sociological categories' (ibid.: 4459).

It is important to mention that the sociological notion of class is a hierarchical categorisation of people where they may share conventional means of production and economic interests. In a highly stratified society like that of Sripuram, these characteristics and patterns are different for the diverse caste groups. This is sociologically important

*Originally published partially in *Sociological Bulletin: Journal of the Indian Sociological Society* 63 (2), May–August 2014: 302–13.

as 'the life of an individual cannot be adequately understood without references to the institutions within which his biography is enacted' (C. Wright Mills, as quoted in Lareau 2003: 14).

Deprivation is not always material, and the non-material domains have been overlooked in mainstream literature. The present work considers conceptualising the voicelessness and powerlessness of the poor as their capabilities deprivation. This deprivation from an intersectional perspective has had a corrosive impact on the Pallars in Sripuram due to their socio-economic marginalisation. According to Sen (1999b):

> What the capability perspective does in poverty analysis is to enhance the understanding of the nature and causes of poverty and deprivation by shifting primary attention away from *means* (and one particular means that is usually given exclusive attention, viz., income) to *ends* that people have reason to pursue, and, correspondingly, to the *freedoms* to be able to satisfy these ends. (Ibid.: 90)

This has been well-established in the capabilities literature. For instance, Nussbaum (2011) argues that:

> [p]overty involves heterogeneous failures of opportunity, which are not always well correlated with income; moreover, people in positions of social exclusion may have difficulty converting income into actual functioning, so income is not even a good proxy for capabilities. In general, income is a means to an end, and capabilities are the end. (Ibid.: 143–44)

In this context, the present study of the social construction of capabilities attempts to understand common aspects like household characteristics and consumption patterns of the different caste groups in Sripuram. Other aspects like livelihood dependencies often provide a clearer picture of the extent of class positions. As a sociological study, this book adopts observational research as its data collection method. Hence, the identification of the poor has mainly been based both on income and non-income factors. This is done following the literature which understands the insufficiency of income as the only factor affecting poverty (see Béteille 2003; Harriss 2007; Kannan and Raveendran 2011; Saith and Wazir 2009; Sen 1999b, among others). For instance, according to Harriss (2007):

> Mainstream poverty research – even after experts had generally accepted the need for multidimensional view of poverty that goes beyond income/consumption measures to take account of holdings of assets and hence of longer run security – has generally failed to address the dynamic, structural and relational factors that give rise to poverty. (Ibid.: *i*)

It is pertinent to note that decrease in poverty over the years is often understood as an effect of neo-liberal economic policies without appreciating the historical and social processes behind it. This signals the fact that the poor people's existence in society often tends to be ignored by the 'official' figures. The multi-dimensional social deprivation conceptually questions the homogeneous economic categorisation of the poor in India. However, mainstream analyses (Jha and Jhingran 2005; Kannan and Raveendran 2011; Thorat 2007; Tilak 1999, 2007) still hold the predominance of the income-based definition as the identification of the poor in the country. This is not conceptually helping the poor. To quote Sen (1973: 1457): 'The Indian poor may not be accustomed to receiving much help, but they are beginning to get used to being counted. The poor in this country have lately been lined up in all kinds of different ways and have been subjected to several sophisticated head-counts.'

There are many practical difficulties in the identification process. For instance, the oft-cited criterion of asset-ownership to identify the poor is not useful in Sripuram, as no one belonging to the erstwhile higher castes (Brahmin, as in the present case) in the village own any land. Hence, for the purpose of this study, sociological literature has been consulted for the process of identification of the poor.[2] In an objective sense, relative deprivation describes 'situations where people possess less of some desired attribute, be it income, favourable employment conditions or power, than do others' (Drèze and Sen 1999: 16, in *Poverty and Famines*).

In Sripuram, the sense of deprivation among the Pallars varies across generations. Most of the older folks view their deprivation either as a functional necessity because of social stratification, or simply their *vidhi* (karma or fate). This is in sharp contrast to the present-day youths who are more assertive owing to the influence of a favourable political economy. The increased levels of education among the younger generations and their exposure to the outside world allow them to question the historical injustices of the caste system. These beliefs are mainly being shaped by the mass media and political leaders in the state.

The other markers of human deprivation, such as housing conditions, standard of living, livelihood insecurities, etc., provide guidelines to identify the poor.[3] People's personal attempts to not 'appear shamefully in public' (Sen 1999b) often proved challenging for the author during fieldwork. For this reason, the present work draws from the ethnographic advantages of disattending to make the poor comfortable with the author's presence in their cultural setting. This was made possible by living in the village during the different phases of the fieldwork.

The definition of 'poor' in this study has been thus based on the identification of livelihoods. For instance, economic poverty and socio-cultural marginality of the villagers, along with deteriorating housing conditions, emphasise that the poor occupy the lowest rungs of the social hierarchy, and that it is socially inherited and perpetuated (D'Souza 1979: 10). The present research is based on observation as well as questioning of the poor about their definitions of well-being and poverty, instead of trying to fit them into the definitions and standards set out by others. According to *Poverty and Social Exclusion Survey in Britain* (2000), it is important to understand poverty as people's subjective notions of being poor, having a relatively low income and lacking socially perceived necessities (David Gordon, as quoted in Wolff and de-Shalit 2007: 110).

Social complexities often obscure the visibility of the poor in the village. Domestic workers (who are mostly women) and casual labourers (mostly men) make their 'humble' presence less visible. Caste–class dynamics pattern their economic dependency on the village social structure. In Sripuram, as Brahmins and Pallars occupy opposite positions in the caste structure, it is not difficult to locate the extremes in their social class positions as well. In other words, the identification of a rich Pallar is as easy as that of the poor Brahmin in the Agraharam. The latter, whose social standing is relatively high in comparison to that of the former, '... is a case in which the human capital of the parents, at least as measured traditionally by years of schooling, is low, but the social capital available to the family for the child's education is extremely high' (Coleman 1988: S110).

The problems of subsistence also reflect the economic realities of the village, providing a picture of the social capital and aspects of mobility. Since habitus determines the a/symmetry of opportunities, this study is an attempt to observe the everyday life in the village to gain insights into the dynamics of poverty and affluence. The author has explored the situations of the poor, who do not have any means to sustain themselves during periods of unemployment despite their education, and also of the members of the local orphanage, which highlights another layer of deprivation in Sripuram.

Besides, the alienation of people from the common property resources, for instance, is not fully quantifiable. The lack of a voice as well as lack of welfare characterise the condition of the poor in the village. We know that the quality of public resources has a lasting impact on the well-being of the poor. For example, as discussed in Chapter 4, the inferior quality of school education in Sripuram has limited the development of capabilities and functionings formations among its residents. With the non-poor leaving local schools in search of better quality education, the 'narrative imagination' (von Wright 2002) of this social re/production has provided a sub-cultural capability-set. Thus, '... the suffering of the poor may depend on the condition of the non-poor' (Drèze and Sen 1999: 10, in *Poverty and Famines*).

When individuals are faced with extreme poverty, both economic constraints and humiliation are experiential social realities that cannot be quantified. These have an impact on the educational functionings and capabilities formations. For instance, Unterhalter has reported about Nigeria that even small things like not having washing powder justify the child's exclusion from the school.[4] Thus, the present framework conceptualises poverty as capabilities deprivation, and raises the question: What does education mean to the poor in their poverty? This is essential as 'there is a danger of seeing poverty in the narrow terms of income deprivation, and then justifying investment in education, health care and so forth on the ground that they are good means to the end of reducing income poverty' (Sen 1999b: 92).

Poverty and Education

The link between poverty and education is complicated. It has been analysed differently in the existing literature.[5] For instance, 'the problem of underachievement in education is essentially a problem of poverty and economic backwardness is not correct' (J. B. G. Tilak, in Rustagi 2009: 64). Although this is supported in a part of the literature (see Banerji 2000; Bhatty 1998a), others have observed that children of low-income families are less likely to be enrolled in school than children of better-off families (Jha and Jhingran 2005: 22). Amidst these different academic positions, we get confirmation that poverty affects the process of socialisation. This, in turn, negatively influences education as well as occupational outcomes.

According to the capabilities perspective, the role of education in development is both intrinsic as well as instrumental in nature. It is intrinsic due to its value as an end in itself; in other words, being educated itself is a mark of development. It is instrumental because it is a means to gaining employment. The educated are expectedly better placed in the labour market than the uneducated. Hence, any research on the poor people's developmental opportunity automatically focuses on education. Despite formidable constraints, 'education seems to provide the best hope for overcoming poverty and vulnerability. The speed of change has been faster wherever the educational attainments are higher' (Sengupta, Raveendran and Kannan 2008: 59).[6] This is also true in the reverse, where 'poverty and vulnerability is closely associated with low levels of education and informality of work status' (Kannan and Raveendran 2011: 60). There is a close correspondence between poverty and vulnerability, and educational incapability (ibid.: 69).

The poor people's dependence on 'fee-free' government schools in Sripuram, which are notorious for their quality standards, necessitates research on functionings. The question is: Is poverty the sole factor determining the educational outcomes for the poor in Sripuram? Ethnographic observations of the lives of the poor in the village underline that although education is seen as one of the essential means of upward mobility, the Brahmins in Sripuram approach it to sustain their social status along with economic mobility. By contrast, others, including the OBCs and Pallars, seemingly view education as a chance at economic mobility. This reinforces the view that 'there is no uniform trend regarding the demand for education among poor and deprived groups' (Jha and Jhingran 2005: 288).

The belief of the poor in education differs across social class. This is due to the structural influences where individuals' preferences are institutionally shaped. For this reason, the Brahmin poor are better placed than the economically deprived belonging to the other castes. The effort to break the cycle of unemployability, therefore, also differs across diverse caste groups. The upper castes, Brahmins in this case, are able to study the labour market trajectories with the result that parents often send their children for extra-curricular training, besides regular college. This may include enrolling them in typewriting or shorthand courses, which are now increasingly replaced with computer courses. These efforts are mostly 'voluntary' in nature. By contrast, the Pallars' decision to send their children to college is a 'luxury'. Furthermore, there is a serious gender differential as well, with some poor Pallars thinking of education as unnecessary for women. For them, 'the short-run opportunity costs of education are perceived to be greater than the uncertain future benefits' (Ayres and Simon 2003: 224).

These diverse educational realities, altogether, denote the definition of quality as far as market-centric notions like employability are concerned. Given the close correlation between caste and economic status, Hill, Samson and Dasgupta (2011: 102) write that '... the private schools tend to be dominated by higher caste groups, although there are examples of low-income families managing to send their children to private schools'.

This contrasts with the social reality of the poor whose futures are affected by primitive modes of production and their inability to compete in the labour market. Migration to nearby towns (mainly Meenakshipuram) is the only developmental option open to the poor youth of Sripuram. The children's engagements with relative and absolute forms of poverty and inequality have had grave implications on their education. For these reasons, the poor in Sripuram do not have any option other than to make education a competitive ideal. As they do not have systemic or structural opportunities to address the complexities of their deprivation, they approach education competitively. This is in line with the human capital approach. This, from the perspective of the capabilities approach, empirically disproves the ideals of education in line with intrinsic notions of education for the sake of enhancing agency-freedom. The poor seemingly approach education to acquire skills. This is in contrast to the central arguments of the capabilities approach and its conceptual critique of the instrumentalism of the human capital ideals in education.

Educational Outcomes for the Poor

The central analysis of this chapter is based on two essential groups in Sripuram whom the author has identified as 'poor': the orphan children and the EUYs.[7] The orphan children are socio-economically impoverished and dependant on the orphanage for sustenance.[8] Their deprivation is due to the demise of one or both of their parents or a broken family structure. All of them come from extreme socio-economic hardship. Although they are fortunate enough to get membership of this institution, their deprivation is manifold. The identification as well as definition of the second group, the EUYs, is based on the framework of Jeffrey, Jeffrey and Jeffrey (2010). These young people are aged between 18 and 35 who have been unable to find employment despite having diplomas, Bachelor's degrees, and in some cases Master's degrees as well.

For this observational research, the individual cases have been chosen based on their class positions (for an overview, see Table 5.1). For instance, the youth who are unemployed from poor households have been given preference in the analysis due to the central aims of the research. Their conceptualisation in a category similar to that of the orphan children has allowed the author to contextualise poverty in Sripuram in a holistic manner.[9]

Table 5.1 EUY and EUEY Respondents in Sripuram: An Overview, 2012

Respondents	*No. of People*
EUYs (5 male and 5 female)	10
EUEYs (8 male and 5 female)	13
Orphans (4 each–2 male and 2 female children–from the 6th, 7th and 8th standards)	12
Teachers (14 + 2 vocational teachers)	16
Opinion leaders	10
Total	61

Source: Author's fieldwork.

The Orphanage

Sripuram has two educational institutions, namely the orphanage and the local middle school. The orphanage is a place where socio-economically deprived children live to 'educate' themselves, primarily at the local school or in the nearby villages. As a 'total institution', the orphanage functions with organisational regimentation; since it departs from basic institutional arrangements, there is a mounting incompatibility with the wider society. The everyday lives of the residents, for instance, are 'structured' by the management. The dominant role of the institution lies in directing aspects of the children's lives. Their everyday interactions and schooling are 'shaped' by the institutional rules and regulations. The constraints on the orphans by the broader society, and the Agraharam in particular, add to the complexity of their social status.

The social exclusion of the orphans is an invisible form of discrimination. This is due to the active role of the state in addressing only visible forms of exclusion through anti-discriminatory laws in the country. The children's adaptive preferences have structured their sub-cultural habitus within the institution. The institutional demands, in Goffman's (1967) notion, 'mortify' the inmates, which in turn 'structure' the self of the orphans. As this 'total institution' restricts the presentation of the self of the children to the ends 'desired' by the institution, the latent structure and processes are thus 'formalised' by the institutional regulations.

The management controls all aspects of the everyday routines of the children, reproduced daily with a few exceptions.[10] On holidays, the children are 'allowed' to visit their parents or relatives. The management controls preparations of food, as well the children's activities like sleeping, bathing and playing inside the institution. It also includes monitoring their 'interaction order' with the society outside. Although the orphanage is situated 'inside' Sripuram, it considers the society within which it is set as the 'outside'. This notion is inculcated among newcomers, who are strictly institutionalised to these role-expectations.

The dependence of the children on the orphanage underlines the institutional inadequacies of unsupportive welfare regimes. Hence, their livelihoods must be conceptualised in terms of their educational functionings and capabilities formations. Institutional failures can be seen in the lives of the old pupils, and the orphans are aware of their inferior educational endowments and inherited inequalities. This is mainly due to opportunity deprivations in their lives. This re/produces weak conversion factors.[11] Also, this is capitalised by the everyday demands of both the local school administration and the orphanage management. The two influential families that run the school and orphanage order children to do household chores at will. This further pushes the children to societal margins. This marginality is further re/produced in the school due to negative stereotyping by teachers, thus strengthening the poverty–illiteracy continuum. Parental poverty, however, compels the orphans to be mute spectators of this 're/production'. Some of the parents consider this a trajectory of 'growth'. The economically deprived, who are also most often socially excluded, perceive their children's 'affiliation' to the influential families as an enabling condition for functionings and capabilities formations. The notion of enabling conditions, discussed in the capabilities literature (Unterhalter 2003b; Walker 2003; Walker and Unterhalter 2007), is essential for sociological reasoning.

The Orphan Children

The institutional linkages between orphanage and the local school are significant. Although the orphanage is owned by a woman, whose husband runs it, it was founded by the school management. Over the years, the school management has sold it to others to unload the administrative burden, most of which arises out of apprehensions over the legal implications of missing children.[12] The clientele of both institutions is mostly poor. This is simply because '... it is not unusual to come across villages, in which the local government school caters primarily to the poorest ...' (Vasavi 2009: 135).[13] The orphanage, for instance, caters to the needs of children who have lost either one of their parents. As these children come from families that have undergone extreme economic hardship, they get an automatic entry into the local middle school. Their 'educational stay' is assured till they finish their studies (up to the eighth standard). Although some of the children get an extension to stay on for a few more years to finish their schooling up to the higher secondary level in Meenakshipuram, this is often at the discretion of the orphanage management.

The development processes through which a child becomes an adult are limited at the orphanage. The near-absence of a welfare regime disables the important avenues of conversion factors in their everyday lives. The 'functional' head of the orphanage is also a full-time teacher in a nearby village. In addition to role-conflicts such as these, the absence of essential amenities in Sripuram provides a weak infrastructural base for the children. Their social vulnerability is further increased due to inferior cultural capital and family poverty. This places them at the social margins in the initial years of their lives.

Social Class Differences

Children's engagements with forms of poverty and inequality have grave implications on their educational outcome. One can observe their everyday educational encounters, mainly regarding adaptive preferences, which gradually push them out of the learning system. This is true for the Pallar children in Sripuram. Even though the local Pallar children are not from the orphanage, their occupational outcomes over the years have been minimal, similar to those of the orphans. This highlights the fact that the social background of the children determines their educational successes. As differences in social class in the children's life experiences can be seen in the details of life (Lareau 2003: 35), it is pertinent to look at the social structure as well. It reveals that parents from different social backgrounds differ in their conception of and involvement in the children's education. This in effect shapes both the educational outcome and social capital. Thus, the expectations from education across social groups are shaped by the caste–class dynamics in the village. In case of the orphans, negative stereotyping, for instance, affects their experiences as well as expectations from education. The broken family structures that these children come from, in this context, compel them to take up institutional membership as a relief from their economic conditions. This temporary economic relief is in contrast to the established claim that parents across all social classes 'pay close attention to their children's education' (ibid.: 198). This could be because '... children from the least well-off families do not have a fair chance at attaining the level of economic security most other families manage to attain' (Bowles, Gintis and Osborne Groves 2005a: 1).

This highlights the urgency to 'understand the individually insignificant but cumulatively important ways in which parents from the dominant classes facilitate their children's progress through key social settings' (Lareau 2003: 278). In contrast to this, there is an additional dimension to the social structure where the OBCs and the Pallars are withdrawing their children even at 'the slightest indication of failure or poor performance' (Sarangapani 2003: 29). The children's engagements with relative and absolute forms of poverty and inequalities thus have grave implications on their educational outcome.

The Institutional Dimensions

The impact of orphanhood on education as well as the institutional role in the functioning of the children are crucial for capabilities formations. As there is a significant risk that orphan children may remain poor even in adulthood, this has implications for their capabilities and well-being. The functionings failure in education is determined by the diverse intersectional factors of parental death, inferior institutional services and insensitive social milieu. The future of orphan children, as well as the present status of capabilities formations, has relegated them to an 'underclass' in Sripuram. Social stigmatisation, for instance, is primarily due to their poverty-stricken orphanhood. However, there are some rare cases where extreme poverty pushes children into the orphanage despite the presence of their parents. These children are considered 'lucky' to be admitted to the institution as it is shockingly competitive for the poor in the nearby villages to gain entry. The parents of these children reportedly use their 'social capital' to influence the management for admission. The institutional membership of these children shapes their socialisation as 'orphans' in Sripuram. Though this is a rational economic strategy for the poor, some of these children are unfortunately socialised as 'orphans' even without parental tragedies.

A majority of the children have lost either one or both parents, but those who have lost mothers tend to suffer more permanent adversity (Beegle, Weerdt and Dercon 2010). Almost all children come from families marked by the severities of economic poverty. Their diverse caste backgrounds along with 'economic unfreedom' (Sen 1999b), to a significant extent, homogenises them to create a 'collective conscience' in the orphanage. The sub-cultural interaction in the institution exemplifies these 'collectivities'. The institutional failures of both the local school and the orphanage have been visible in their 'lifetime welfare loss' (Beegle, Weerdt and Dercon 2010: 163). While the failure of the orphanage is mainly due to successive 'welfare' regimes that are unsupportive, the school is notorious for the poor 'quality' of its education. Thus, the institutional sufferings range from orphanage regulation to inferior schooling, which create a web of deprivation for the children. Their physical presence at the institutions becomes a waiting period to escape to the uncertain world outside. The agonising trauma is reinforced by the socio-economic backgrounds of the inmates. The higher the age, greater the chance of becoming a pessimist. An informal interaction of the author with the orphans confirmed this. For instance, the older children were more apprehensive about their future than the younger ones. The consequence of this is that the pessimism of the older children often makes in-roads into the psyche of the younger children.

In addition to these failures, institutional socialisation at the orphanage generally reinforces the social construction of gender. Structural forces operate so that everyday roles are 'assigned' according to sex. The sexual division of labour, for example, allocates 'hard' manual works to boys. The girls, in contrast, are assigned to take care of 'softer' roles like cleaning and caring for the younger residents. This social re/production very often perpetuates stereotypical gender values inside the institution. The normative structures of the management ensure this perpetuation of stereotypes. The children who are subservient to the management's never-ending demands are naturally the 'preferred inmates'.

As a result, they become a reference group for the anticipatory socialisation of the newcomers. Considering this, institutionalisation regulates the adaptive preferences of the everyday encounters of the orphans in Sripuram. The children are expected to be in the institution according to the temporality of the day. Non-school hours are spent inside the orphanage. This normative structuring ensures neither educational attainment nor their 'active' participation in the orphanage. In consequence, social exclusion is institutionally re/produced in their everyday lives.

Though schooling is not merely about keeping students inside the institution, the common bureaucratic approach to education ('educracy') firmly believes in disciplining the children. While individuals do have their ways of learning, institutionalism of this nature is hardly sensitive to diversities. This is due to the conventional belief that students are a homogeneous group to be 'moulded' according to the educratic guidelines. At the institutional level, both the local school and the orphanage function on these beliefs. One cannot entirely blame the children for their subservient status in the bureaucratic hierarchy, or for their inability to find possible avenues for 'innovation'.

The orphanage, however, has institutional 'autonomy'. This is seemingly due to the inactive role of the state. Given their young age as well as the strict institutional structures, the orphan children do not have avenues of agency formations. They perceive themselves powerless in everyday institutional encounters. In addition to this capability deprivation, neither institutional support nor family care is available to them. This has severe implications on their well-being; the support available to them in the name of social welfare is cosmetic and minimal. Their educational outcome from the local school is also very minimal. This, in turn, fails them in almost all aspect of their lives.

Processes of social inclusion are unsuccessful due to the isolated institutional presence of the orphanage in the village. Villagers in Sripuram try to keep a safe distance from its financial dependencies. This distancing process happens across all caste groups. Weak financial and functional support from the state as well as people's negligence negatively influence the capability formations of orphan children. This often leaves them at mercy of philanthropists.[14] Due to these cumulative disadvantages, one cannot see the enormous change in their educational outcome both in the past and the present.

Lastly, the systemic expectations of manual labour from the children are often taken for granted. This is because of their vulnerable status; they suffer multiple disadvantages, especially when they are from the erstwhile lower caste groups in the orphanage. In addition to this, even for the school administration and the secretary's family, the orphan children are the preferred servants to be 'employed'. This is mainly because no one questions this form of socialisation when they see the youngsters working as 'unofficial' peons.

Quality Concerns

Based on the preceding discussion on social class differences, it must be mentioned that:

> ... schools bring little influence to bear on a child's achievement that is independent of his background and general social context; and that this very lack of an independent effect means that the inequalities imposed on children by their home, neighbourhood, and peer environment are carried along to become the inequalities with which they confront adult life at the end of school. For equality of educational opportunity through the schools must imply a strong effect of schools that is independent of the child's immediate social environment, and that strong independent effect is not present ... (Coleman et al. 1966: 325)

The orphan children, in this context, are most often neo-literates from a broken family. As the school and the teachers 'are not equipped to cope with children who are first generation learners in their families' (Banerji 2000: 801), they do not learn anything valuable for the future. There is a discrepancy between 'the learning at primary schools and the lived educational experiences ...' of the children at home (Singh 1995: 735). This is not due to the institutional structures of the village; the problem lies somewhere else. The state's welfare policies are not proactive enough to take care of society (Venkataraman 2018c). For instance, indifferent implementation of the education policies without any intention to genuinely improve their lives could be the main reason. The recent incidence of politicisation of the textbooks in the Samacheer Kalvi (Education for All) system in Tamil Nadu is an illustration to be noted. The contestations between the dominant political parties in the state have added additional layers of complexities in education.

As the '... children of more highly educated and economically successful parents tend themselves to complete more schooling and earn more ...' (Duncan et al. 2005: 23), the failures of the orphan children are often seen as 'normal' in the village. For instance, barring a few reported exceptions, none of the children from the orphan school gain secure employment. These institutional failures are, however, viewed merely as failures of individuals. This underlines the fact that the enabling conditions of institutions mostly determine the occupational outcomes of the education. Though intersectional variables like caste and class are also important, institutional failures over the years have reinforced the status quo in newer forms.

Thus, systemic inadequacies and structural exclusion due to socio-economic stratification cumulatively push the orphan children to the margins. The result is that their persistent struggles against opportunity deprivation encircle them in the trap of everyday social exclusion. Given that the process of graduating into adulthood from childhood is mainly shaped by educational institutions, it must be noted that any qualitative failure at the school level is costly in terms of capabilities formations. In this context, the agency-goal formation of the children in a government school is expectedly inferior due to the non-poor migrating out of the local school system. The 'narrative imagination' (Nussbaum 2006) of this social re/production provides a sub-cultural capability system in Sripuram. This puts the orphan children at a disadvantage 'both because they inherit lower endowments and because capital constraints on their parents limit the market value of the endowments that they do inherit' (Becker and Tomes 1986: S16).

Thus, the intersections of the caste–class dynamics and institutional inadequacies reveal the complexities of the social construction of capabilities. This intersectional sociological reality has often been overlooked in India. In the words of Lareau (2003: 64): 'Social scientists interested in determining the dominant factors shaping children's lives are often preoccupied with a hunt for single determinants—they hope to be able to point to, for example, the overriding importance of income *or* education'. Thus, the central focus should be on knowing these complex factors from the home and the school that put children at a disadvantage.

The Sripuram orphanage caters mainly to the needs of the local middle school. The local school, for instance, is functionally dependent on the orphanage for its yearly enrolment drives; the non-poor leaving the local school has made it easier to accommodate the poor. For this reason, the orphanage has become the main stakeholder in the local school. However, the management alone cannot be criticised for the unsupportive 'welfare' regimes; one can observe the formalism of the institutional regimentation which separates the orphanage from the wider society. Though the orphanage as a 'total institution' physically exists in the village, its 'social distance' is relatively high.

For this reason, the educational failures of the orphans are perceived to be less valued when 'normal' children themselves are struggling for outcome in the village. The impacts of institutionalisation can be seen in the children's behavioural, emotional and intellectual disorders. Along with a dysfunctional family background, these disorders shape their attitude towards life.

Lastly, it must be mentioned that institutional gatekeeping ranges from the management's continuous refusal to grant access to the official figures of the inmates to their unwillingness to allow the author 'inside'. This, however, motivated the author to see the institutional dimensions from a 'distance' in the village. Occasional opportunities allowed the author to observe its everyday functionings. The orphans who were studying in the local school were prompt in allowing those windows of opportunities. The informal interaction with the children outside the orphanage, in the end, has provided a detached picture. This picture has been re/produced without being 'channelled' through the gatekeepers. For instance, the author's enquiries about the alumni revealed shocking institutional insensitivity. Neither the school administration nor even the orphanage management had any idea about the orphans who had graduated over the years. Their failure to keep track of the 'gone cases' is justified in their educratic formalism.

Against this backdrop of discussing the conceptual linkages of poverty and education in developing the central arguments of the social construction of capabilities, it is pertinent to discuss the educated unemployed youths in Sripuram. It must be mentioned again that aspects of 'economic unfreedoms' regarding poverty have been conceptualised in light of both the orphan children and educated un/underemployed youths. The following section discusses the educated unemployed youths in Sripuram to analyse their adaptive preferences.

Educated Unemployment

Educated unemployment is a disincentive for the education completion rate. In India, the social capital theory has convincing answers for differential educational outcomes. This is because the outcomes in education are higher for the erstwhile higher castes, primarily because of their ascriptive inheritance of 'knowledge' capital. This is true even if they do not have an adequate occupational outcome.

They are able to pursue temporary working arrangements through vocational routes in order to survive in the absence of opportunities and choices. Underemployment must be conceptually analysed within the unemployment framework. This newer framework is also based on the conceptual appreciation of the fact that the underemployment of the educated youth hides the severities of unemployment in their everyday life.[15]

As there have been very few attempts to examine the coping strategies that educated young people adapt to negotiate unemployment in India, the present framework attempts to understand the distribution of unemployment in each social group in Sripuram despite its education status. The everyday lives of the educated unemployed have provided the clue for quality and capability debates in education. During fieldwork, the educated unemployed youths were asked: Why must one be educated? How has your ascriptive status (like caste membership) helped you in securing employment? How has your educational qualification helped you gain entry into the formal labour market? How confident are you of breaking the cycle of poverty through education? Moreover, who helps you with finding a job?

These broader questions have further been driven by the two central concerns of capability formations: How does education help in everyday life? Moreover, does education allow one to take decisions independently? In Sripuram, the cultural differences in learning become an explanation for the educational failures. In school education, the poor are often left with lesser life-chances because of the low quality of learning. This has been well established in the literature: inferior quality provides a weak social capital base.[16] Also, a familial history of economic depravity has ensured a weak habitus. The result is the vicious cycle of deprivation with lower educational outcomes. Because of this, the transition of the poor to the formal labour market is not smooth.

Thus, traditional professions like agriculture become an option for the educated youth who fail to find any other employment in the village. Manual labour in the unorganised sector is also preferred because of its informal economic nature. Upadhya (2007) argued that Brahmins are better placed in the labour market than those from other castes. Natesan, for instance, is Brahmin by birth whose education has failed him. He has been forced to work in the informal economies in Meenakshipuram. Brahmins are mostly known for their relative educational successes, but Natesan's economic deprivation on account of a failed education system has made it difficult for his father to find him a bride. Thus, Natesan, who works an unsecure job, is a negative reference point in the Agraharam. In a visit to Sripuram in 2012, the author found that Natesan had lost his job in Meenakshipuram.[17] This reiterates the central argument that the working status of the educated unemployed youths is vulnerable due to labour market volatilities, resulting in increased dependence on their families for socio-economic sustenance.

Also, the failure in the occupational outcome is not present only among the educated. In Sripuram, the educated unemployed often also work in jobs that are below their calibre. Due to this, they are insecure about their future, given the informal nature of the economy (of the unorganised sector). The educated underemployed are mainly functional illiterates. This means that even though they may hold a qualifying certificate, they often do not have the functional literacy or skills in their field of study. For instance, Raman, a Commerce graduate was not aware of the basics of his subject when we discussed it during casual interactions. This is similar to the case of Iyappan (see Chapter 4) who has more degrees in hand than anyone in Sripuram. He struggles to analyse even the common issues. However, most of these dysfunctional literates are not willing to take up manual work (in agriculture, for instance) owing to its perceived inferior value in the village economic system. Thus, the presentation of the self in everyday life (Goffman 1959) is structured around economic failures. Consequently, they mostly rely on all possible avenues in the informal economies in Meenakshipuram.

Reflexive observation of the educated unemployed further underlines aspects of structure and agency in Sripuram. Individuals' negotiation as an agency with the structural constraints of the 'knowledge society' often compels the former to keep accumulating degrees until they get formal employment. While there is no growth avenue for personal economic development, 'individuals often resort mainly to education. This socio-economic process is often called fallback strategies' (Jeffrey, Jeffrey and Jeffrey 2010). This, in turn, makes people approach education primarily for its employment prospects. Any failure in this approach pushes them to the edge (see Kieselbach et al. 2001). The prolongation of education for employment and the earning handicaps due to chronic unemployment offer important insights into understanding poverty in Sripuram.

Given the informal nature of the economy, the uneducated are less affected by the unemployment issues in Sripuram. Even though the educated unemployed are often unwilling to take up manual work, most of them consider these as underemployment based on their education and class positions. Consequently, they keep waiting for 'better' opportunities. Those in abject poverty cannot, however, keep waiting for too long. The case of Selvam is pertinent here. Selvam is a 22-year-old non-Brahmin male with a Bachelor's degree in Business Administration. Despite his qualification, he has not been able to get a salaried job and is forced to work as a coolie. His underemployment status highlights the differential education outcome due to his ascriptive status in providing the lack of choice in 'opportunity sets'—this, in turn, creates an unequal social structure. Differentially distributed resources extend this inequality across social groups in the village. As a result, the lack of opportunity further encircles capabilities deprivation in the social structure of Sripuram.

Also, the skill pressures on human agencies are very much historical. In the present phase of globalisation, the nature of skill pressure on human agency is high in a different form. Anyone who is not well-qualified to market oneself cannot even dream to survive. The educational functionings have, therefore, mainly been treated based on their the human capital implications on individuals' lives.

The suffering of the educated unemployed youths in Sripuram is seemingly due to personal as well as systemic failures. Infrastructures as well as curricular and pedagogic limitations are becoming barriers for agential growth. For instance, Kumar, an unemployed youth belonging to the OBCs, one of the Dominant Castes of the village, made use of his ascriptive status to enter local politics. His regular visits to the panchayat office allowed him to enter the closed networks of the panchayat president. This proximity to the village political elite was not automatic: his ascriptive status played an important role. However, he gave up his political attempts in 2010 and started working as a security guard at a bank in Meenakshipuram. His politico-economic failures have revealed that the status of being unemployed despite having educational qualifications questions the very notions of self-identity. Hence, the theoretical notions of capabilities will not serve any valuable purpose until one gets a livelihood. This also underlines the methodological importance where the status of being unemployed is dynamic due to labour market volatility.

Nature of Educated Unemployment

The nature of educated unemployment has been categorised into two central aspects in this work: institutional and individual. The qualitative interviews[18] with the educated unemployed youths and observation of their lives have revealed that (i) occupational mismatch; (ii) credential gap; (iii) functional illiteracy; (iv) qualification escalation; and (v) skill loss are important institutional factors in their lives. Though these five features are determined by institutional factors, their active interaction with the individual or personal factors complicates the nature of educated unemployment. Personal factors include: (i) family poverty; (ii) fatalism; (iii) dispirited searches; and (iv) disinterestedness to work (Figure 5.1).

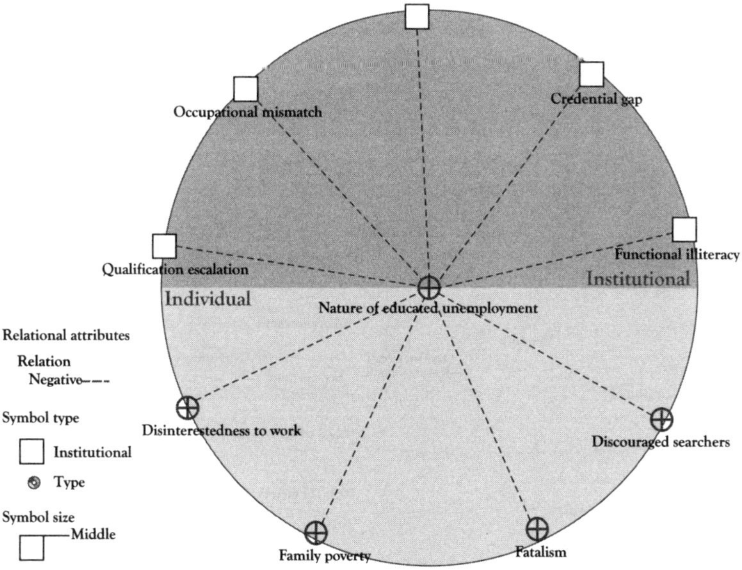

FIGURE 5.1 Nature of Educated Unemployment: Network Map

Source: Created by the author.

This intersection of institutional and personal factors, as mentioned earlier, runs across caste, class and gender domains where the intangible roles of the social structure can intersectionally be conceptualised. The interaction among the various features is negative where power and privileges are often re/produced in everyday life. This provides the details of the social construction of capabilities in the village.

Causes of Educated Unemployment

Against this background, the central causes of educated unemployment can broadly be categorised into three domains. In the institutional domain, one can observe the factors of (i) dysfunctional education quality; (ii) credential gap; (iii) absence of institutional interactions; (iv) institutional dependency of the individuals, both voluntary and involuntary; and most importantly (v) corruption (Figure 5.2). These factors, with their active interaction, institutionally reinforce the causes of unemployment among the educated youths in the village.

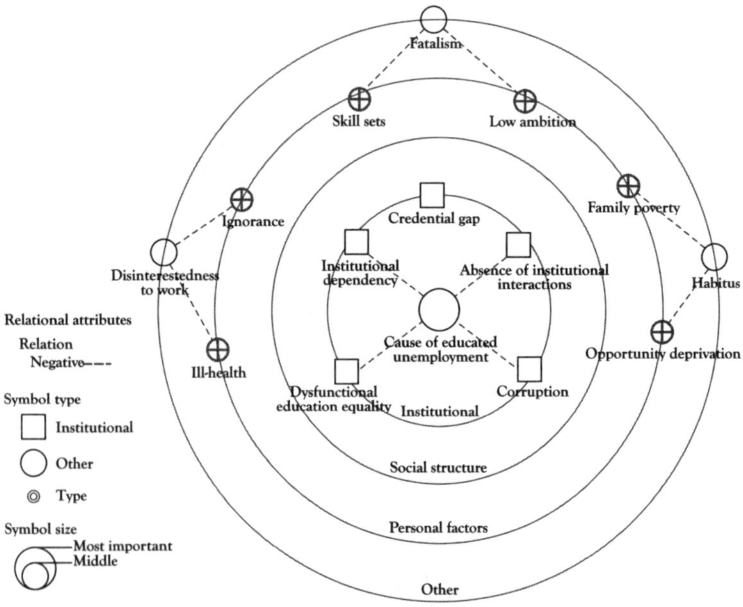

FIGURE 5.2 Causes of Educated Unemployment: Network Map

Source: Created by the author.

Also, personal factors such as (i) family poverty; (ii) ill-health; (iii) ignorance; (iv) low ambition; (v) absence of skill sets; and lastly (vi) opportunity deprivation push them to the economic margins. These six factors can be conceptually placed between the institutional and social structural influences in the village. However, there are other factors like fatalism, disinterestedness to work, and the habitus, which essentially complicate this intersection. The everyday interactions of these factors reinforce the deprivation trap of development. The absence of institutional interaction, for instance, pushes the youths to be system-dependent where corrupt practices often get institutionalised.[19] For instance, the case of Iyappan can be seen in light of his 'rationale' for getting a salaried government job. Also, a systemic factor like dysfunctional education ensures the credential gap where the individual agency does not have functional literacy. Similarly, family poverty with its habitus ensures opportunity deprivation where individuals' self-esteem takes a back seat.

Everyday Life of the Unemployed Youths

The living pattern of the unemployed youths highlights the potential reasons for as well as effects of their un/employabilities. A typical day begins differently for the male members of the different caste groups. For instance, Vasu (39) and Natesan (36), both Brahmin EUYs in the Agraharam, begin their day at six in the morning with newspapers and coffee. This is followed by the usual routine of bathing and breakfast. Then the 'working' hours begin with their plans to go to Meenakshipuram 'to do the usual work like purchasing groceries or going to the bank for the family'. This takes half a day, after which they come home for lunch. The regular afternoon nap follows. They receive their evening coffee immediately as they wake up. They then sit outside to observe the street sometimes. This is followed by planning their evening; they bathe or merely wash their faces to go to the nearby temple for the day. They chat with friends and acquaintances in the locality in the evenings. They then take refuge in television, to watch the news to 'update' their knowledge. They wait for dinner, prepared by the women of their family, while watching drama serials on television. Once dinner is over, they do not 'waste' time sitting inside their homes. The usual chats with the neighbours continue until it is time for bed.

In contrast to these Brahmin youths, the OBCs and SCs spend their normal day somewhat differently. It generally begins at seven with the noises of the schoolgoing children in the locality. After brushing their teeth, they go to a tea stall on most days to read the daily newspapers with coffee or tea. Then around 8.30 a.m. some of them go to the nearby 'field' to excrete. If the day is expected to be busy, they bathe there in the common pond and come home for breakfast. Then the 'tough' time starts. Either they must join their peers in the street to plan for the day, or go to Meenakshipuram to roam around. Normally, they do not come home for lunch if they are in Meenakshipuram as it takes some time to reach Sripuram. If the day is 'successful', some of them go to the nearby theatre to watch a film to pass the time (Jeffrey 2010a). Sometimes, they come back for lunch and sleep in the house. The evenings are quite 'lively' with the return of the working men and women from the fields and from other odd jobs in Meenakshipuram. The everyday interactions about the day and politics occupy most of their time in the evening, which is followed by the dinner.

An observation of the unemployed as well as unmarried women's everyday life gives the impression that their days are generally 'the waiting period to get married'. Their family members also expect them 'to get ready' by learning culinary skills and caring for their future children. A typical day of the Brahmin women, as well as OBC and SC women, who are not working, is different from that of the men. Their entire day is full of demanding work in the kitchen. They are expected to get the children to study. If they find free hours, most of them spend that time worshipping at the local temples.

Irrespective of caste and class factors, present-day technologies are playing a crucial role in passing the time. These include television and mobile phones. Through these, the youth are relatively more aware of goings-on in the world than the preceding generations in the village were. These technologies, therefore, contribute to their social capital formation to no small extent. Though some of them (mostly the OBCs and SCs) may have the inferior habitus due to intergenerational illiteracy and poverty, these 'modern' communication gadgets make them confident to face the day-to-day challenges. The emergence of an interaction order out of these instruments of freedom at times increases their independence in making their decisions. Though this may be against the established patterns of society, it seems that smaller avenues of this kind provide them with the conversion factors for their capabilities formations.

Everyday observation of these individuals reveals the nature of the education system and its uselessness in their daily lives. Although every one of them is differently educated across diverse castes in the village, none of them finds their education useful enough to actualise their living. It seems that the only purpose of education is to help them to read newspapers in the morning 'to form their opinions' on the local public issues. Beyond that, most of them expect help even for the usual tasks at the banks or in other government offices. The government's rhetoric on the enrolment drives and infrastructural investments in successive policy notes has overlooked the importance of quality. The functional aspects of education have generally been ignored. This is a sad social reality at a time when education becomes the only possible route in addressing the uncertainties of underdevelopment.

The process of modernisation structurally pushes out the misfits who refuse to walk with the times. The role of education with its differential outcome across diverse social groups in the village reinforces the deprivation trap. This vicious circle has, however, been predominantly analysed at the institutional levels. However, the intersectional aspects of this trap and its complex social reality have to be explicitly highlighted. The observations on the orphan children and educated unemployed youths in Sripuram have thus revealed the role of the social structure in the educational outcomes of human agencies. This has a futuristic implication where there is a positive correlation between rising unemployment and the inferior educational provisioning of the government. Mainstream employment research must conceptualise this nucleus aspect. Thus, ethnographic evidence of the poor people has highlighted the secondary educational outcome and its effects on the capability gaps in the village. Observations of everyday interactions and coping strategies of the poor in their socio-economic spheres have therefore provided valuable insights not only about education and poverty, but also about the social construction of capabilities in Sripuram.

NOTES

1. See, for instance, Ayres and Simon (2003); Aturupane, Glewwe and Isenman (1994); Banerji (1997, 2000); Bebbington (1999); Béteille (1972b, 2002, 2003); Cleaver (2005); Collins (2005); Connell (1994); D'Souza (1979); Deaton and Drèze (2002); Drèze and Sen (1999); Fonseca (1971); Gang, Sen and Yun (2004); Gupta (1984); Harriss (2007); Jha and Jhingran (2005); King, McGrath and Rose (2007); Laderchi (2001); Levine (2004); Mendelsohn and Vicziany (1998); Saith and Wazir (2009); Sen (1973, 1999b); Thorat (2010); Thorat (2007); Tilak (1999, 2002a, 2002b, 2005, 2007); Tooley (2004); Tooley and Dixon (2007); Townsend (1954); White, Leavy and Masters (2003), among others.

2. The 'cultures of poverty' arguments of Lewis (1998) as well as the relative deprivation theses of Townsend (1954) are a few of the related conceptual leads on the subject.

3. Though the nature of these social factors is external to the individual, they constrain their behaviour.

4. At the International Conference on Children's Capabilities and Human Development: Researching Inside and Outside of Schools at the Faculty of Education, University of Cambridge, Cambridge, UK, on 11–12 April 2011.

5. See, for instance, Ayres and Simon (2003); Banerji (1997, 2000); Connell (1994); Jha and Jhingran (2005); King, McGrath and Rose (2007); Tilak (1999, 2002a, 2002b, 2005, 2007); and Tooley (2004); Tooley and Dixon (2007), among others.

6. In Sripuram, unfortunately, economic alienation of the EUYs has increased despite their educational attainment (see Chapter 4).

7. For a detailed discussion on the EUEYs, see Chapter 6.

8. The orphanage is a distinct institution in Sripuram that primarily serves the local school. Although it is privately managed, it gets some ir/regular financial support from state and central ministries. It primarily serves children who do not have either one or both parents.

9. As part of this ethnographic study, the author collected primary data from the village of Sripuram, with a focus on 61 individuals for the current research objectives. The details of caste and gender are given in Annexures I–III.

10. These children often do not have the usual opportunities to go out even on holidays. Their visits are decided by the management on a case-to-case basis.

11. Conversion factors, according to the capabilities approach, represent how many functionings one can get out of a good or service. For the discussion related to social reproduction, see, for instance, Willis (1977).

12. At times, the children run away due to their inability to stay away from their respective (broken) families and friends.

13. According to Hill, Samson and Dasgupta (2011: 102), 'Given the close correlation between caste and economic status ... the private schools tend to be dominated by higher caste groups, although there are examples of low income families managing to send their children to private schools.'

14. Since the enrolment figures of the local school depend on the children from the orphanage, the school secretary indirectly offers donations either by way of food or other essential commodities. This is among the numerous acts of philanthropy that support the orphanage throughout the year.

15. The central arguments of EUEY have been discussed in detail in Chapters 6.

16. See, for instance, Dyer (1996a); Kumar (2004, 2007); Kumar and Sarangapani (2004); Mehrotra and Buckland (2001); Naik (1979); Nussbaum (2006); Støren and Aamodt (2010); UNICEF (2000); Velaskar (2010), among others.

17. In the last telephonic conversation with Natesan, which took place on 25 September 2013, the author found out that he had not yet found another job. A follow-up about him with others in 2018 revealed no change.

18. The audio-recorded interviews of the EUYs were transcribed with the help of F4 software. These were further coded in Atlas Ti for analysis and depiction through VennMaker (see Figures 5.1 and 5.2).

19. On a related note, this aspect has been empirically discussed in Chapter 6, which discusses adaptive preferences.

six

Adaptive Preferences and the Social Construction of Capabilities

The present chapter analyses caste, class and education of the EUEYs. Based on ethnographic fieldwork, it examines the role of education and its outcome across diverse social groups in Sripuram. The sociological analysis highlights the capabilities and functionings formations of the youths. Observations of the coping strategies of the EUEYs in their socio-economic spheres provide insights into both education and poverty. This naturally has a futurological implication where there is a correspondence between rising un/underemployment and inferior educational provisioning of the Indian state. This chapter thus discusses the nature of educated underemployment; the adaptive preferences of the EUEYs; and the social construction of capabilities considering their functionings failures in Sripuram.

Educated Underemployment

The definition of underemployment focuses on the failed efforts of the educated youth in obtaining a salaried job. It considers how their economic necessities push them to take up any job instead of idling time away or waiting for better opportunities. Jeffrey's (2010a: 2) discussion of the 'culture of limbo' seen among educated unemployed youths, for instance, considers the conception of the period of un/underemployment as a 'waiting period'. This chapter specifically discusses underemployed youths and their involuntary or unplanned breaks from the labour market. Thus, youths aged between 18 and 35 years represent functionings failures on account of their inability to gain salaried employment. These failures, given the grave implications they have on their well-being, are analysed as 'evaluative spaces' of the capabilities approach (Robeyns 2005). These spaces, namely functionings and capabilities, are decisively influenced by the intersectionality of caste and class positions of the human agencies both in education and employment.

The inabilities of the EUEYs to secure white-collar jobs, which often connote 'development', leave them with low-quality employment. Their subjective rationalisation regarding their adaptive preferences creates a reserved 'army of labour' in the informal economies. Barbara Harriss-White (2003: 17), for instance, reported that the informal economy accounted for nearly 93 per cent of the workforce in India. This workforce neither had any social welfare benefits nor was it covered under the legal-economic frameworks. Its livelihood was often left to the mercies of the market. Thus, the forms of underemployment are mostly visible as inadequate employment that is involuntary. Against this backdrop, this chapter probes the conditions under which education dis/empowers the human agencies in Sripuram. This is conceptualised keeping in mind the possible conversion factors in intersectional arrangements. The notion of intersection is conceptualised as how the structural characteristic of caste and social class interacts in capabilities and functionings formations of the EUEYs. Thus, the central argument underlines the 'temporal anxieties' (Jeffrey 2010a) in highlighting the nature of social arrangements under which the EUEYs are shaping their personal and collective agencies in the village.

The coping strategies of the EUEYs from the perspective of the capabilities approach explain their adaptive preferences and 'agency-freedom' (Sen 1999b) in Sripuram. The work-lives of these youths, it must be noted, represent a continuum between underemployment and unemployment. For instance, Nirmala's (a 27-year-old Pallar woman) transition between different jobs keeps her unemployed even during the short periods of underemployment. It must be noted that despite severe socio-economic constraints, Nirmala has a Bachelor's degree with 'higher' levels of typewriting skills both in English and Tamil. She is often forced to take up any job available to support her aged parents. This highlights the fact that the transition from education to employment is not automatic. The deterministic intersectional factors can be observed in the functionings and capabilities of the

EUEYs. As lack of access to training and employment has been a critical factor in underclass formation (Faist 1993: 309), the systemic inadequacies in terms of quality predicaments and policy failures need to be underscored keeping in mind its adverse effects on the educated youths in the country. The EUEYs of the current research highlight these effects in their coping strategies.

The re/production of privileges mediated by intersections of caste and class dynamics is an important sociological issue. The village represents the prevalence of primordial identities in contrast to its 'modernising' rhetoric. As these identities are dynamic, considering numerous factors including education and economic mobility, the intersectional analysis underlines the newer forms and nature of caste and class. Sripuram represents one such village in Tamil Nadu where the primordial notions are evolving according to newer social realities. This evolution is understood as the combination of both internal and external social forces when considering the dynamic complexities of the social orders.

Considering these complexities, the intersectional process of employment must be understood in terms of its implications for capabilities deprivations. The constant underclass formation due to social reproduction through education in employment conforms to weak conversion factors. The consequence is visible in the EUEYs who are mostly from socio-economically vulnerable households in the village. This underlines the fact that education ensures them neither capabilities to live a life according to their personal choices, nor the functionings to approach everyday economic un/certainties. Thus, the notion of education confirms the thesis of 'degrees without freedom' (Jeffrey, Jeffrey and Jeffrey 2010) in Sripuram.

The challenges of employment, given these constraints, are high among the Pallars and the OBCs in Sripuram. For instance, the OBC women, even if they are educated like the Brahmins, are neither allowed to step out of the village in search of salaried employment, nor able to find casual work like the Pallars. This is due to structural restrictions where 'family honour' or caste predominates. For instance, Sunitha, an OBC woman, is not able to find a job outside Sripuram despite having a postgraduate degree with various skill sets. Even though she is aware of the possible economic avenues in getting salaried employment, her adaptive preferences limit her within the borders of Meenakshipuram.

Her parents' concerns of 'safety and security' of women have restricted Sunitha's socio-economic mobility.

Considering these self-subordinations, the everyday lives of the EUEYs either become 'waiting periods' for marriage, or they fatalistically hope for a natural transition to the next stage to happen. Thus, the absence of access to both salaried opportunities as well as informal economic livelihoods questions the very relevance of education. This often leaves women dependent on the male members of the family, typically the father and elder brothers (until one of them gets married). This leads to economic exclusions where women EUEYs are pushed to the extreme margins due to patriarchy. Also, access to salaried opportunities is formalised to recruit qualified 'matching' candidates. This systemically excludes the neo-literates and the socio-economically deprived. These first-generation educated wo/men often do not have the disposition and interpretative skills; their habitus and social capital do not seemingly match the market demands. Thus, their inability to match the anticipatory roles keeps them out of the economic capital.

Furthermore, even the informal economy recruits new employees through local references. This reinforces the hierarchy where the plum posts are allocated according to societal powers and privileges. In this context, economic marginality of the erstwhile lower castes like that of the Pallars can be seen. For instance, given their perceived social status, if a Brahmin applies for a similar job where youths from other castes have also applied, the former's chances of getting the position are higher in the informal economies, mostly due to the image they have cultivated through their vegetarianism or teetotallerism. Thus, the incidence of unorganised work status is generally 'higher among lower social status groups' (Sengupta, Raveendran and Kannan 2008), with a few exceptions.

The prevalence of underemployment, therefore, manifests the complexities of unemployment. This requires that underemployment of the youths also has to be conceptualised as disguised unemployment in Sripuram. In this complexity, one finds an institutional vacuum in terms of public responsibility regarding avenues of job training for the educated youths. For instance, the District Employment Office, or 'Employment Exchange', though situated in the headquarters of every district, does not seemingly serve any purpose when it comes to providing information on the various career opportunities. It ritually registers job seekers and 'uses' their details to keep a Seniority List, according to government policies. Against this backdrop, it is important to mention a local youth's opinion on the institutional ir/relevance of such agencies. Karthi is a 24-year-old OBC EUEY with a Bachelor's degree in Business Administration:

> LAKSH: Did you register yourself in the Employment Office?
> KARTHI: Yes, I did. I registered my qualification once I completed the 12th standard.
> LAKSH: Did you find it useful?
> KARTHI: To my knowledge, no ... They may send an Interview Card when one turns 60 or 70 years (of age). So, it is of no use in real life. (Interview from the field, dated 18 October 2011.)

In this context, one must note that in the neo-liberal economic order, there are fewer government jobs (*arasaanga velai*). For instance, India has seemingly left the school-to-work transition to the mercies of the market and its self-regulation. This unfortunately re/produces social privilege through education in employment. Social re/production, considering the intersectionalities, retains caste underclass formations. The Pallars of Sripuram are an example of this formation where the mal/distributions of life's chances provide the markers of capabilities deprivation. Against this backdrop, individuals' underemployment should also be conceptualised as a socio-economic dysfunction. One reason for the persistently high social inequality among different caste groups with regard to access to quality education and employment is public policy. The nature of policies is such that they are often targeted based on ascriptive identities in India. In addition to this, there is no institutional support for training the non–university goers, with a few exceptions like the Industrial Training Institutes (ITIs) and diploma colleges. This has systemically resulted in a situation where the country is one of the highest educated un/underemployed regions in the world (*Outlook* 2018; Varghese 1989).

Entry into the labour market in India is mostly based on the quality of institutions the individuals attend. This is due to the segmentation of educational credentials at the systemic level. The 'superior' quality education services are inaccessible to the poor and the socially disadvantaged. Competitive entry into these institutes is reliant upon the economic and cultural capital of the applicant, which makes them inaccessible for the poor. Considering these lesser life-chances, education is a reproductive avenue of power and social privileges where erstwhile lower castes like the Pallars inherit the inequalities in Sripuram. The relative disadvantages of the OBCs in general and the Pallars vis-à-vis the Brahmin youths in overall unemployment have, however, decreased over the years, though at a plodding pace. This decrease is mainly due to the accommodative opportunities of the informal economies in the absence of active employment policies (Jeffrey 2010a).

Consequently, the constant failures mentioned regarding the functionings of EUEYs and regarding underclass formations have grave implications for the broader notions of capabilities in the country. This underscores the fact that individuals' economic success is mostly dependent on his/her ability to embrace modernity. Education as a crucial factor of modernity most often fails the poor in its promises of capabilities formations due to lack of access to quality institutions. The non-poor people, who are predominantly the Brahmins of Sripuram, are, however, able to better their life-chances by focusing on education-based economic mobilities. Also, an interesting aspect concerning the Brahmins in Sripuram is that their social class positions do not limit their qualification escalations. In other words, there are no marked differences in the educational strategies of the poor and non-poor people Brahmins in the village. This could be due to their socio-histories of treating knowledge as a capital. Set against this background, the competition to garner the opportunity-sets for salaried employment and the complex socio-economic factors of qualification escalation highlight 'invisible' contestations of castes in re/producing newer forms of inequalities. These forms can be described in their adaptive preferences.

Adaptive Preferences

The concept of adaptive preference, according to Elster (2016), is based on the 'sour grapes' phenomenon: 'Ah well, it's more than likely they're not sweet–/Good only for green fools to eat!' (Jean de La Fontaine, as quoted in Greene and Elffers 1999: 301). This can be described as the human agency self-subordinating its beliefs. In contrast to this, the capabilities approach concerns agentic resignation to extreme deprivations. The ongoing debate in the literature revolves around the considerations of justifying adaptive preferences regarding the rational or irrational resignation of the individuals (see Bridges 2006; Bruckner 2009; Khader 2009, 2012; Teschl and Comim 2005; Watts 2013). Considering these diverse positions, this chapter analyses adaptive preferences with respect to subjective rationalities.

The concept of adaptive preferences has been analysed from 13 qualitative interviews of EUEYs as part of this fieldwork. The data has been segregated with the assistance of Atlas.Ti where the coded items have been thematically organised. Consequently, it has delineated the aspects of the EUEYs' lower occupational expectations; 'adjustments'; fatalism; fall-back plans; and the changing career trajectories due to non-availability of matching jobs. Also, the subjective labour market experiences of the EUEYs in light of socio-economic exclusions underscore how employers' expectations shape the EUEYs' preferences and expectations formation in the village. This is further conceptualised in terms of endowment differences of individuals in their social class positions, which are visible in their educational functionings. The autonomy deficits of the EUEYs and the absence of choices highlight their economic hardships, agential rationalities, relative deprivation and coping strategies. These issues have been discussed in detail here.

In Sripuram, the unequal patterns of employment and mobility among equally qualified social groups underline the fact that the intersections of caste and class continue to be a potent predictor of capabilities. The 'functionalities' of the adaptive preferences can be observed in the keenness of the EUEYs to cultivate their networks. However, this often rationalises white-collar 'deviances' like the ability to make use of 'recommendations' and other monetary 'considerations' as enabling conditions for entry into the labour market. The notion of recommendation is colloquially referred to as 'reference' or 'intro' in the village. An individual's ability to get a 'favour' decides not only their formal selection, but also their access to information about the vacancy itself. This highlights the fact that information is a scarce capital in the village. For instance, Muthu, a 23-year-old OBC male with a Bachelor's degree in Business Administration, works as a casual labourer in the informal economy:

> LAKSH: What kind of hurdles do you face in reaching your goal of working at a company in an appropriate position?

> MUTHU: I do not get a job wherever I go. No one responds positively. After the interviews, they just send me out. I do not even know where the jobs are available. English and Computers have become necessary for every role. They expect a lot from us. (Interview from the field, dated 20 October 2011.)

Access to the 'inside track' is planned by economic or political means. These considerations highlight the excessive bureaucratic demands and corruption. The bureaucratised institutions working for education and employment systemically overlook their role in addressing the 'human flourishing' (Nussbaum 2006). This, from the perspective of the capabilities approach, is an important conversion factor which needs to be sociologically theorised. The liberal frameworks of the capabilities approach in general and the conception of adaptive preferences must be carefully analysed in collectivist societies like India where individuals most often represent themselves in terms of their primordial identities of family, caste, class or all of these together.

Further, agency choices are restricted by paternalistic social structures. For instance, the aspirations of the EUEYs are at times scuttled in the name of 'duty' and 'respect' for one's parents. The debilitating conditions of systemic oppressions are complicated by the patriarchal family systems and paternalistic social structures. In this context, let us look at Raman's case. Raman is a 35-year-old Brahmin male who completed his Bachelors in Commerce along with other skill training courses like typewriting and computers. Despite these qualifications, he has failed to get a job. He 'adapted' his preferences in employment by capitalising on his ascriptive status as a Brahmin in the village. He started working as a priest by facilitating rituals (*vaitheeham*) for other members of his caste. Even though he took this up in a casual manner in the initial years, his inability to get salaried employment has turned priesthood into a full-time job.

> LAKSH: So, due to unexpected failures, you initially started *vaitheeham* as a side business?
>
> RAMAN: Yes [frustrated tone], now the bylane has become the main route.
>
> LAKSH: How confident are you about this work? About its income and growth?
>
> RAMAN: I cannot visualise it. Somehow it is fetching some money. It gives some hope.

> LAKSH: Did you get support from anyone in the awkward situations you have explained earlier? I mean, from friends?
> RAMAN: None. Everyone went on with their own lives. No one helped me during my difficulties. I had to stand on my own. No help at all. (Interview from the field, dated 26 October 2011.)

Though this highlights the complexities of functionings failures due to economic constraints, it is essential to analyse the deprivations of the EUEYs of the other castes in the village too. For instance, in contrast to Raman's economic unfreedoms (Sen 1999b), the Pallar EUEYs like Mala, Nirmala and Mahesh (mentioned later) underscore a complex web of functionings failures and social exclusions. These complexities analysed from the perspective of the capabilities approach highlight the reinforcing of intersections of class and caste factors. Given these social intricacies, it is pertinent to conceptualise the subjective rationalities of the EUEYs in the village.

Subjective Rationalities and Coping Strategies

The subjective rationalities of the EUEYs in light of their adaptive preferences highlight the issue of corruption as agency rationality, that is, an individual's ability to rationalise a particular decision. This is contrary to the moralistic positions where individual rationalisation considers these to be 'enabling' conditions. Against this backdrop, it is important to mention Nirmala, who has multiple socio-economic constraints: those of being a woman in a patriarchal social order, and of living in the village with severe infrastructural and opportunity deprivations.

> LAKSH: So you mean to say that all are appointed through bribe?
> NIRMALA: Yes. Money is a crucial factor. Otherwise, you need to have political influence. Through these things only one gets a job these days. (Interview from the field, dated 2 November 2011.)

Considering the twin factors of money and political influence, the availability of information itself is capital—a scarce one, however, due to the economic constraints and rural habitus of the EUEYs. The rationality formations, in this context, overlook the deterministic roles of the macro-economic forces in their lives. For instance, though most of the EUEYs reasonably escalate their qualification by upgrading their clerical skills, these trainings are dysfunctional. Although learning typewriting can help them work fast, it is not useful, considering their practical inabilities to operate computers. The cultural capital of the lower class youths remains 'outmoded and redundant' (Deuchar 2014: 110). Their economic constraints prevent them either from learning computer operations or even from training at good quality institutions. This is generally due to the high fees of these institutions. Consequently, these subjective rationalities have to be conceptualised as the EUEYs' coping strategies.

In Sripuram, socio-economic limitations shape variations in coping strategies of several castes. Though some of the Brahmin families have severe economic constraints, they generally do not have concerns about social exclusion. This is naturally due to their erstwhile higher status in the social hierarchies. Brahmin EUEYs like Raman and Jayanthi (see Chapter 3) are relatively better placed in comparison to the others. In contrast, Pallar EUEYs like Iyappan, Nirmala, Mahesh and Mala underscore the deprivation trap. This should be seen in the intersection of adaptive preferences and coping strategies. For instance, Iyappan (see Chapter 4), despite being an economically well-off EUEY with multiple educational credentials, does not have the required financial and social dispositions.

In contrast, Jayanthi, who is 10 years younger than Iyappan with similar educational qualifications, has the confidence and disposition to make use of her skills and credentials. Although both Jayanthi and Iyappan were working as contract teachers at nearby government schools in 2013, differences in their 'clarity' to escalate their education credentials are seemingly different. The role of the family and neighbourhood in habitus formation is a key factor. Jayanthi's residence is adjacent to those of the locally influential villagers. This indeed provides her with the enabling conditions for capabilities formations.[1]

In contrast to guidance from her educated family members, Iyappan's neighbourhood is notorious for regular street fights and alcohol addictions. This is in addition to widespread illiteracy and unemployment where their everyday socio-economic dependencies are on others, including the OBC landholders or Mirasdars.

Thus, the coping mechanisms of the EUEYs, despite their educational credentials, differ due to the intersectional factors of class and caste. That the EUEYs in Sripuram neglect to upgrade their skill sets—their ability to operate computers, for example—proves to be a costly error. These errors are determined by class and caste positions where exceptions like Jayanthi can be found only among the erstwhile higher castes. Men from the higher caste have better chances of enhancing additional skill sets because of family habitus as well as socio-economic capabilities.

Thus, economic uncertainties on the one hand, and the hard manual labour required in agriculture on the other, are forcing the EUEYs to stick to their efforts to gain salaried employment. Their failure to land white-collar jobs leads them to work in the informal economies. The adaptive preferences of the EUEYs in Sripuram should be understood taking into account these economic constraints. The job insecurity of the informal economies, and also the everyday struggles in finding work in Meenakshipuram, make the EUEYs anxious to enter salaried white-collar jobs. The nature of capabilities deprivation is furthered by psychological issues, for example, Raman's complaints about his inability to sleep at night. Furthermore, the effects of relative deprivation and economic unfreedoms combined with social exclusion strengthen the capabilities deprivation of the EUEYs. Against this deprivation, it is essential to discuss conversion factors.

Corruption as a Conversion Factor

Corruption is rationalised as an 'enabling' condition in Sripuram. For instance, Iyappan's efforts at 'arranging a job' signify the extent of the justifications. His frequent usage of metaphors in describing corruption confirms it as an essential conversion factor. Iyappan's 'awareness' of the need to arrange Rs 8–9 lakh for a teaching position in any management school highlights the current 'market rate' in Tamil Nadu. In his view, this rate may also increase in the future. Ethnographic fieldwork allows for the understanding of a sensitive issue like corruption. As a native speaker, the author picked up on subtle references to corruption, which was indirectly referred to as 'something', 'paisa', 'deal' or 'to correct' by the EUEY interviewees. Raman's rationalisation can be understood in this context:

> Raman: I think, we need to give "something" even to clear the exams ... Yeah, not in thousands, one must bribe them in lakhs [of rupees]. Only then can one click it.

> LAKSH: Does anyone you know "have" it like this?
> RAMAN: I heard about it in Tanjore, as others were talking. I am yet to meet them. (Interview from the field, dated 26 October 2011.)

On the necessity of money in recruitment, Raman's views resembled those of the others in the village. For instance, Nirmala shares: 'For 12 vacancies, they invited 57 people for the interview. My sister also went, but other people got it after paying a bribe. So she came back empty-handed' (interview from the field, dated 2 November 2011).

Although this systemic reality is appalling, the author's effort to understand the complexities of corruption exposed a few other broader aspects:

> LAKSH: Do you think that one cannot get a job without money?
> IYAPPAN: Of course not! Money is the determining factor today. For the opportunities coming out of Employment Office, we generally do not need money now. But the positions in the management school or in any other place are mostly determined by money.
> LAKSH: Any other means?
> IYAPPAN: Appointments in all the aided schools are mostly by money, mediated through political connections ... No one appoints us simply because we have a qualification matching the available job. It will be determined by the amount we bribe them (Interview from the field, dated 28 October 2011.)

In addition to these affirmations, Raman's regular visit to the District Employment Office highlights the mundane plights of the EUEYs. He says, 'I offer them some tea or snacks in the nearby shops to get the necessary information. What to do? We can get inside information only through these means so I politely collect it over tea' (interview from the field, dated 28 October 2011).

Considering their agentic dependency, there are variations across departments and sectors whose nuances need to be discussed. For instance, in its drive to make a profit, the private sector may not compromise on the recruitment quality of the employees. However, the very information about the forthcoming vacancies is generally circulated within the closed network. For instance, Karthi admitted that:

> Even I did the wrong things. For instance, when I was working in a company, and there was a vacancy, instead of advertising it,

> I just passed the information within my known circle of friends and took one of them on. Today everyone does the same in his or her workplace where the outsiders may not even get the information about the vacancies. (Interview from the field, dated 30 October 2011.)

Similarly, Sundaram, an EUEY who influences others through his political activism, argued:

> LAKSH: Is systemic corruption in the government the primary reason for the low quality of education?
> SUNDARAM: It is also a corruption.
> LAKSH: What kind of corruption can one do in government schools?
> SUNDARAM: Non-performance of the assigned duty for which one draws a salary itself is corruption ... People work hard till they get a government job. They abruptly stop working once they get it. This is because of their insensitivities. (Interview from the field, dated 3 November 2011.)

Thus, rationalisation of corruption and nepotism is prevalent across all castes, with rare exceptions. The youths of Sripuram are influenced by new political outfits like Naam Tamilar (We, the Tamils). This is actively shaping behaviour through debates, with a referencing of Tamil cultural pride. This is in contrast with the previous generation which spends their time in mundane 'casual' activities in Sripuram. The present-day youths are influenced by Sundaram's political activism, and his regular news updates from various sources like the television, internet and newspapers. Thus, his coping period is seemingly being used for political actions in the village. The systemic barriers faced by the EUEYs and the inefficiencies of the bureaucracy, like the ones Sundaram mentioned, add a dimension of systemic corruption, underscoring the severities of opportunity deprivations.

Opportunity Deprivations

In the socio-economic sense, the everyday lives of the villagers of Sripuram depend on the nearby town of Meenakshipuram. Villagers rely on Meenakshipuram to meet their basic needs including education and health. This can further be understood with regard to the infrastructural concerns where villagers do not have the local economic options for growth and development. Agriculture is the dominant mode of production, and there are economic constraints on the poor. Mala aptly summarises the situation in Sripuram: 'It seems that the nature of suffering is such that the people's opportunity to even find food now seems to be scarcer than in the past' (interview from the field, dated 7 November 2011).

The very notion of opportunity deprivation can thus be observed in the socio-economic constraints of the villagers. This is in addition to the livelihood necessities which put pressure to emigrate to the greener pastures of the nearby towns like Tanjore or Chennai. Kumaran, a 23-year-old OBC EUEY male, articulates his concerns as follows:

> LAKSH: It seems there is no employment opportunity available in Sripuram.
> KUMARAN: Yes.
> LAKSH: The village exists by merely depending on Meenakshipuram ... In that situation, what kind of hurdles do the youths face here?
> KUMARAN: Due to family poverty, everyone needs money. So, the youths are not able to study ... Also, families are not compelling the youths to study. No one does it. The youths fetch some money by working odd jobs. Though they initially do it for fun, they slowly drift away from their studies. Naturally they regret this later in life. Generally, no one here realises that education is essential ... They realise it very late in life. (Interview from the field, dated 5 November 2011.)

In this context, the everyday struggles of Mahesh throw further light on these severities. Mahesh is a 24-year-old Pallar EUEY with a Bachelor's degree in Business Administration. He describes his attempts at getting salaried employment:

> There are plenty of interview communications lying at home. I get calls from so many companies like Silicon Water Solutions, etc. I have applied to multiple places where they ask me to meet them directly with all the certificates. If I need to go there, I must have 1,000 rupees for travel expenses to Chennai. The same will be the case for Coimbatore as well ... Due to severe financial constraints, I reject these calls myself, instead of following the normal practice like the other applicants do [awkwardly tittering] ... Their invitations are just lying at home. (Interview from the field, dated 9 November 2011.)

In this context, it is pertinent to discuss the relative notions of deprivation. Relative deprivation is a conception of an individual's self-experiences of being deprived of something to which they believe they are socially entitled. This is sociologically significant in understanding how the EUEYs perceive their adaptive preferences in the village. For instance, Iyappan, one of the highly 'qualified' youths with a diverse set of skills, in response to the author's query regarding his failed efforts at gaining salaried employment, asked: 'What else can I do?' Assertions like these underscore the complexities of deprivation, where Iyappan represents the socio-economic marginalities. This is important in his case since he is a member of the Dalit community. This can be contrasted with Raman's (a Brahmin youth) assertion that: 'I need to struggle a lot even for the trivial things in life.'

If we look into the statements of two individuals, Raman and Muthu, whose everyday struggles are representative of those of the EUEYs in the village, we see, first, that the marginalities of the EUEYs can be observed in their public invisibilities. This could be due to their conscious attempt to not 'appear shameful' in light of the economic successes of others in the village. Raman, for instance, compares his struggles to get salaried employment with those of his peers. This signals opportunity as well as relative deprivation where he feels he would be able to climb the ladder like the others if he had better chances in life. His emotional outbursts often blame his earlier decisions as being 'idiotic', where he feels bad about the jobs that he did not join. This agony questions the very relevance of education in shaping individuals' choices and opportunities. In contrast to Raman's self-blame, Muthu's views of his family's poverty relate to the prosperity of others. He says that 'we are at the platform' (meaning his family does not have any social opportunities), despite the prosperity of the neighbourhood. Though this underscores the relative deprivation, it is essential to underline that some of the EUEYs are self-critical in their outlook. This can be observed in Muthu's attempt to contrast the present with the past:

> My family was destitute but now we are slowly growing. This is because my brothers and I are working now. Earlier, we did not even have food three times a day. We were attending the school essentially for food. We go there to at least get one meal a day. (Interview from the field, dated 4 November 2011.)

These two factors, that is, family poverty and deprivations, reconfirm the fact that most of the EUEYs do not have personal choices due to their 'unfreedoms' determined by the intersectional social factors of class and caste. Raman again is of the firm view that the relative deprivations of the EUEYs are determined by caste factors in the village.

> RAMAN: There will not be any problem if you are an SC today. In their caste, there may be someone who helps.
> LAKSH: Why is no one helping you?
> RAMAN: In the Brahmin caste, people are self-centred where everyone concentrates mostly on his or her own family. Of course, it is natural. But they should at least show some sympathy for people who are in need like me. (Interview from the field, dated 7 November 2011.)

In light of this depreciative comment, it is appropriate to mention the self-critiques of the EUEYs. For instance, Muthu's opinion of the inabilities of the poor further reveals the nature of deprivation in the village. For him:

> ... people like me, who are going for interviews from the villages do not have all those facilities to improve. However, the people from the town often have opportunities to learn computers even at an early age. Their parents train them in all these things. That is why they come up very early in life. (Interview from the field, dated 4 November 2011.)

The subjective rationalities of the EUEYs and their relative deprivation underscore the necessities to analyse coping strategies in comprehending the social construction of capabilities. Education from the perspective of the capabilities approach argues for human development. However, the functionings failures in ensuring even the basic expectation of a functional outcome question its very relevant. The promises of education are akin to a placebo-like treatment when it comes to functionings and capabilities formations. This is contrary to the Pygmalion effect where the educational functionings can 'reportedly' be influenced by the expectations of others. The failures of functionings formations thus highlight the complexities of capabilities deprivation among the EUEYs to underscore the intersectional social factors in both education and employment. Their economic unfreedom with respect to the aforementioned factors reproduces the powers and privileges where the complexities of capabilities can consequently be seen in their adaptive preferences.

Note

1. The usual constraints of the EUEYs present the complexities of their adaptive preferences regarding deprivations and coping strategies. The author's efforts to know their expectations from the government have provided clues about the issues that are most urgent for these educated marginalised youths. In Mala's view, 'the government should provide good education and create specific job opportunities for the villagers'. Youths from all castes agree with this; a Brahmin EUEY, for example, asserted that people will not leave Sripuram if there were opportunities locally available in the village.

seven

Capitals and Capabilities*

The contestation among the castes in Sripuram is seemingly to control the shrinking resources and economic alternatives in the village. The education system plays an instrumental role in deciding success. Almost all caste groups treat education with instrumentalist human capital notions. Employment-centrism thus seems to provide resistance to the conversion of the human capital approach to the capabilities approach. This is primarily due to the intersectional dynamics of caste and class positions of the poor in the village.

Along with the structural reality, even human agency fails to treat education from the perspective of capabilities. The employment-centric approaches do not assure economic avenues either. The primary reason for this dichotomy between the human capital approach and capabilities framework is systemic, where the quality of education becomes relevant. Against this backdrop, it is essential to understand the aspects of human and social capital in capabilities formations.

Human Capital

The human capital approach considers human beings as agents of wealth production. Accordingly, it approaches skills and knowledge as forms of capital by placing education as an economic good. Globalisation has led to skill-centric market pressure on human agencies

*Originally published in *Youth, Gender and the Capabilities Approach to Development: Rethinking Opportunities and Agency from a Human Development Perspective*, ed. Aurora Lopez-Fogues and Firdevs Melis Cin, 92–107 (London and New York: Routledge, 2018).

in India today. The structural withdrawal of the state from knowledge domains leaves this agency alone.[1] As a consequence, the Darwinian law naturally gets applied, where only the 'fittest' survive. Any notions of capabilities thus must conceptualise the intersecting complexity of the structure–agency dualism as the process of learning becomes a commodity in the market-centric 'knowledge' economy. The pressure to develop skills and its role in competitiveness must be understood in terms of the increasing withdrawal of the state from the globalised political economy. Consequently, structural as well as systemic 'false consciousness' misunderstands the notions of capabilities merely as skills (Venkataraman 2011). This is seemingly 'facilitated' by neo-liberal market fundamentals. Individuals conceive of education as 'investment'. In this context, skills become the tools through which individuals survive in employment. If anyone fails to 'market' their innate abilities and skills, they are deemed unemployable. Thus, educational functionings in India are increasingly being understood through notions of the human capital approach. For instance, the Ministry of Human Resource Development argued: 'The improvement in higher education is being brought through restructuring academic programmes to ensure their relevance to modern market demands ...' (Government of India 2012–13: 58).

Against this backdrop, the status of un/employability symbolises the systemic limitation of education. The inferior quality of pedagogy and curriculum ensures neither broader notions of capabilities nor functionings. The systematic withdrawal of the state from public policy commitments has gradually allowed the labour market to define 'quality' in education (Venkataraman 2016a). These definitions are generally market-centric notions of employability instead of the constructivist ideals of the National Curriculum Framework (National Council of Educational Research and Training 2005) in India. Thus, the social re/production of educational functionings seems to stabilise the status quo in favour of the non-poor people and the erstwhile higher castes. In the neo-liberal economic reality, children in private schools have current learning and future wage advantages over those in government schools. These schools often consider the ideals of human capital as an educational outcome.[2] Thus, the system, in the words of Bowles and Gintis (1976: 103):

> legitimates economic inequality by providing an open, objective, and ostensibly meritocratic mechanism for assigning individuals to unequal economic positions. The educational system fosters and reinforces the belief that economic success depends essentially on the possession of technical and cognitive skills – skills which it is organized to provide in an efficient, equitable, and unbiased manner on the basis of meritocratic principle.

Furthermore, it is to be noted that the inferior educational outcome of the social groups, including that of the erstwhile higher castes, limits their life opportunities to escape these economic unfreedoms. This causes a restructuring of the social roles and status among them. For instance, the increasing un/underemployment among Brahmins compels them to take up the revivalist role of the Brahmaniyam.[3] Although this profession is monetarily not as rewarding, one can see an intrinsic competition among the EUEYs for it. However, recent political discourse has removed the traditional entry-restriction according to caste for this traditional service in Tamil Nadu. For example, the state government under the Hindu Religious and Charitable Endowments Department has decided that anyone can become Kurukkal by pursuing a degree in the institutions which are established by the government of Tamil Nadu.[4] This decision would have been unthinkable during the period of Béteille's (1965a) study, when these jobs were traditionally given to only a particular sect of the Brahmins. This has sent a shock-wave among the Brahmins who are generally known for their orthodox principles. Nevertheless, most of the unemployed Brahmin youths are increasingly taking up the role of Kurukkal in any available temple in their locality without even knowing the subtleties of the Ahamam rules. They often cite reservation policy as one of the 'entry barriers' in the current formal economies.

In contrast, some of the Pallar children who skip school[5] and the unemployed youths are developing a sub-culture. Though this has its version of 'functional' capabilities, agentic efforts to break their deprivation trap and economic mobility are drawn mainly from their educational functionings.[6] For instance, Natesan, a Brahmin EUY with a Bachelor's degree in Commerce, had initially 'succeeded' by becoming an accountant in a small business in Meenakshipuram. Individuals like him are gradually 'marketing' their unemployability for livelihood in the informal economies. This structurally allows them to be 'active' in local affairs such as the Brahmothsavam and other festivals in the temples of Sripuram.[7] Most often these temple activities provide them with the social approval of being a 'good person', as religious outlook is often correlated with character credentials. Thus, educational dysfunctionalities are in/directly accommodated by the informal economies.

Though education-induced emigration provides economic benefits to the local Brahmins, the social structure has additional complexities. For instance, the older generation feels that they have been left behind by their children. While some of them are nostalgic for their earlier status in the caste system, they are also emotionally constrained by their inability to leave the village permanently, like their children. However, emigration is seemingly the necessity when there are no economic avenues in Sripuram. Thus, the younger generation generally moves out of the village as it does not have any lucrative opportunity for developing its socio-economic status. They often live in nuclear families in the nearby towns where they work, leaving their parents in the village. As this is a predominant trend among the local Brahmins, the Agraharam has become an 'old-age home' for the elders left behind.

However, this has not impacted the 'other' castes so far. They rarely leave their elders, as most often their adaptive preferences and agency rationality convince them to search for jobs in nearby towns and to continue to live in the village. It must be noted that adaptive preferences are an individual's self-subordinating beliefs; the educational outcome for them is relatively low. The Pallars specifically stand at the margins of development due to the vicious circle of educational deprivations and inferior cultural capital. For instance, given the same level of education, most of the Brahmin youths work in Chennai with stable jobs, but still 'ambitiously' look for further opportunities.[8]

In contrast, the EUEYs belonging to the OBCs, such as Jeeva, a 31-year-old male from a middle-class family who discontinued his Master's degree in Commerce to assist at his father's tea stall, look for opportunities only within Tanjore. He is yet to find one as he needs to help his father. As the coping mechanisms of the youth are seemingly different, the erstwhile higher castes, given their historicity of knowledge-oriented livelihood, can afford to take the risk of investing their living only on education without getting 'diverted' by mundane issues. However, for others, this seems impossible, except in a few rare cases of 'committed' individuals like Iyappan (see Chapter 4), whose educational 'commitments' are also seemingly due to the support structures available in their families. However, the case of the other Pallars is depressing as their inferior socio-economic status limits opportunities and choices for them in Sripuram.

Against this background, the reservation policy in the government sector is perceived as a way of slowing down the options of promotion for the Brahmins. This is seemingly due to the special quota for the erstwhile lower castes. Consequently, the Brahmin youths concentrate mostly on their functionings by looking outside public institutions. Their employment-centric education 'strategies' are contrary to the ideals of the capabilities approach as their aspirations are predominantly career-centric. They aspire for the 'meritocratic' private sector instead of the human capital approach perspective. Thus, the unsupportive state structure, with poor quality and 'preferential' treatments to the erstwhile lower castes in public institutions, seemingly pushes them towards the private sector. Emerging market-driven neo-liberal economic values where knowledge becomes a 'capital' for the surplus-drive of profit is responsible for this. In contrast, the other castes 'depend' on welfare regimes at 'street-level bureaucracy' (Venkataraman 2018).[9]

The Social Capital of Educated Youths

The notion of social capital is embedded in the resources of the networks that an individual or group has in life. These resources mostly shape the approaches to education as well as its functionings.[10] In the present case, caste-based social capital plays both functional as well as dysfunctional roles. The nature of social capital differs across diverse groups. The educated unemployed, for instance, do have support structures to rely upon because of the dynamics of caste, class and education. However, these youths are seemingly taken for granted in the local affairs in Sripuram. They are expected to be active in village affairs such as festivals or panchayat elections. In addition, there are differential educational outcomes that negatively influence the others in the village. For instance, if an EUY 'roams around' the village aimlessly, the poor instantly rationalise not sending their own children to school at the cost of available economic opportunities. The 'reluctant' justifications often get rationalised according to intersectional family dynamics. Since there are no accurate official records on fertility and mortality rates, both state administration and even the local bureaucrats do not have the precise demographic details of the village. This re/production of 'reasons' often justifies why the poor opt out of learning even at a time when compulsory education is considered a necessity.

Also, the unemployed individuals who are willing to work have to compromise their 'market values' according to their socio-economic status. This is important, given the reality where emigration to the nearby towns is the only 'developmental' choice for the poor. However, those who are unwilling to emigrate out of Sripuram, as is the case with Raman and Natesan (see Chapter 5), will have to compromise their livelihoods. The harsher realities of underemployment are in/visible as most of them depend upon the informal economies of either Sripuram or Meenakshipuram even for small pecuniary benefits. An interaction with Natesan, for instance, revealed that the poor people, irrespective of caste, often do not have the necessary social capital which highlights the complexity of the situation, especially in the time of need.

> NATESAN: I was working in the cycle-mart in Meenakshipuram till 2006. Then my brother had an accident.
> LAKSH: Yeah. He was talking about it the other day.
> NATESAN: Both my father and I were taking care of him as my mother could not do this work. So I spent my entire time on him.
> LAKSH: So you left the job?
> NATESAN: No. I did not leave the job. They told me not to come as I was not able to work regularly. He had to stay in the hospital for three months. No one helped us even at that time. No financial help from the cycle-mart. I was expecting them to help me at least with my future salary. No one enquired about care. Neither my colleagues nor the boss bothered to visit my ailing brother. (Interview from the field, dated 10 November 2011.)

In India, economic deprivation of the poor is generally conceptualised in terms of social exclusion. Though the erstwhile lower castes are at the developmental margins, the poor people, irrespective of caste background, often do not have the necessary social capital. Natesan's case highlights this reality. Also, the economic realities of the poor have a gender dimension, where women are unequally placed in the patriarchal social structure. In this, the role of caste is visible where Brahmin women are relatively better placed than women belonging to 'other' castes in the village. The Pallar women, in contrast, are at the social margins where their livelihood is mostly dependent on the male members of their households. However, there are a few small economic opportunities, such as rearing cattle and casual labour in the nearby agricultural fields, to avoid the deprivation trap. These modest options are visibly insufficient. In this context, Mala, a 24-year-old educated unemployed Pallar woman, opines that:

> To a great extent, people in the village do not have any work to do. They idly sit at home. For me, it seems that the nature of economic suffering is severe at present. I mean, now people's opportunity to find food seems to be more difficult than in the past. Today, people survive mostly due to people like me who are educated only to get something from outside in sustaining the family. (Interview from the field, dated 7 November 2011).

However, Mala's underemployment from a complex social context like that of Sripuram has often been overlooked in India. This is due to the systemic challenge in employment where *even* men fail to get decent jobs at par with their educational credentials. While this highlights the intricate patriarchies, one can notice informal networks which are often formed along caste lines.[11] This general arrangement is often exclusivist in nature due to the stratified social structure. The interplay of caste and class dynamics complicates the formation of these networks. Hence, the structure–agency interactions are mostly influenced by these complications. For instance, some of the Brahmin youths who have left the village for better economic avenues share that they usually help fellow villagers based on their 'levels' of friendship with them. Given their 'superior' cultural and economic status, the social capital of Brahmin youths is higher than that of the others at present. For a non-Brahmin, help generally comes from their sustained associations in the Agraharam. Although no one deliberately does this at the time of economic need, there is a subtle point which needs to be noted. The formation of peer groups since childhood is one of the foundations for developing a wider social network in later years. This is significantly absent for the Pallars because of the structural 'restrictions' where their position is distant from the primordial power centres of the village. Their educational deprivation and secondary occupational outcome perpetuate this even for the privileged few.

In contrast, individuals like Karthi have been actively assisting temple services in the Agraharam. By his own admission, at times, it helpfully places him nearer to the networks in Chennai. Thus, the social capital of the Brahmins is ensured in the Agraharam. The membership in the neighbourhood is mostly ascriptive. This shall be further seen in terms of the social change where the residential patterns are increasingly changing. The economically well-off OBCs from outside are replacing the emigrating Brahmins. Though there are structural tensions between the Brahmins who continue to stay in Sripuram and the newcomers as 'full members' of the neighbourhood, it confirms the complexities of caste today. The economic exodus of Brahmins towards nearby towns facilitates this social process. The result is a newer social arrangement, which is at times 'unacceptable' to the remaining orthodox Brahmins. This can be noticed in their nostalgic preference for the habitus like that of the earlier years with exclusivist lifestyles.

In this social construction of capabilities, it is pertinent to conceptualise habitus as a disposition of the structural factors. In a complex social structure like that of Sripuram, the interaction order lays the foundation for social capital. This, however, cannot ensure the basis for habitus formation, given the structural location of the different castes. Law prevents the visible forms of exclusion, whereas the 'invisible hands', at times, withdraw from the interaction order. Often, this withdrawal itself provides the power to influence others, as it does for the erstwhile higher castes. In simpler terms, no one can legally challenge people of the higher castes if they refuse to interact with other castes.

The changing nature of economic opportunities and caste in its new avatar has led to people leaving the village for employment reasons. However, differentials in education functionings prevent this in some cases due to differences in social capital. For instance, the 'high' levels of educational qualifications of Karuppaiah's daughters, who belong to an OBC agriculturist family (see Chapter 4), have failed them as 'children are strongly affected by the human capital possessed by their parents' (Coleman 1988: S110). Their failure to find salaried employment negatively influences the neighbourhood. These functionings failures and capabilities deprivations can be contrasted with the habitus of Brahmins. Tamil Brahmins, for example, celebrate all the different stages of the life-cycle, starting from birth–*ayush homam* (naming ceremony, called *punniyajanam* among the Pallars and OBCs), *upanayanam* (sacred-thread ceremony for adolescent Brahmins), *kalyanam/vivaham* (marriage), *shashtiabdapoorthi* (marriage celebrations when the groom is 60 years old), *sadhabishekam* (marriage celebrations when the groom is 80), and finally death rites.[12] These are occasions for the kin groups to get together. These rites of passage ensure their social capital; no new entry into this group can be allowed except through ascriptive membership and conjugal connections. However, this aspect of habitus formation has increasingly reduced with the younger generation moving out of the village due to economic reasons and the influence of current urban lifestyles.

By contrast, social interactions among the other castes happen to cross the social system mostly in the Shiv temple in Sripuram. This contrasts with the exclusivism of the Iyengars. For this reason, the Shiv temple provides an avenue for social capital formation, for both Smartha Brahmins and the OBCs. The Pallars are far removed from these institutional opportunities due to their marginal position in the social structure. The modernity and outlook of a caste group often decide its human capital agencies. Though caste as an endogamous unit provides a social capital base, the success or failure of the agencies in human capital is often intersected by systemic and structural interactions.

Also, newer modes of communication, such as television and mobile phones, ensure potential avenues of social capital for the villagers. These were non-existent during Béteille's (1965a) time, but today they consolidate the existing cultural and social capital amidst the contestation of castes. Although the reach of telephones among the social groups reflects their social positions, to a large extent they alter the nature of structural hierarchies. For instance, almost all Pallar households 'proudly' own a handset today. This can be seen even among the poorest of the poor, who often struggle financially to maintain it. However, this gives them a new space to improve their social capital in both the market and non-market spheres of habitus formation.

By contrast, the Tami Nadu state governance and developmental efforts are deficient even in ensuring the basic needs.[13] This has not provided the necessary opportunities of capabilities formation for the poor so far. Thus, the social re/production of inequalities often reinforces the existing arrangements in new forms. For instance, given the stringent anti-untouchability laws, the nature and forms of social capital have increasingly been intangible over the years. However, one can see them in subtle forms where the display of economic success through education, for instance, can often be seen in the nameplates on houses.[14] Their symbolic presence in the streets of Sripuram signals the educational functionings and social capital in general.

Conversion Factors

The social capital of educated youths, or their aggregate network of resources, can broadly be categorised along the lines of caste, family, politics, friends, institution and the village. The web of social organisation plays an essential role in an individual's functionings and capabilities formations. For instance, the standard of living of un/underemployed youths and their quality of life are primarily influenced by their family habitus. In this context, the education of the parents is an important parameter. Social capital formations of the poor are generally determined by the intersection of these aspects, where politics-based local networks and influential 'connections' arise. This is primarily due to individuals' image-making and adaptive preferences in life. Also, in the institution-based avenues—such as career planning—skill formations are shaped by the welfare regimes where reservation policy becomes essential. This can be conceptualised as shown in Figure 7.1.

In this conceptualisation, the nature of the interaction is diverse as the intersections of social capital could be functional to the non-poor, whereas the very same could play against the poor.[15] The result can be seen in the institutional dependencies and adaptive preferences of individuals. The credential gaps of EUYs often push them to the margin where their literacy becomes a dysfunctional factor. Also, it is important to mention the underemployed youths. The case of Iyappan, an individual with multiple degrees, is an instance of 'qualification escalation'. As a Pallar youth, his dispositions are seemingly limited by the intersections. This is important in the present-day welfare regimes

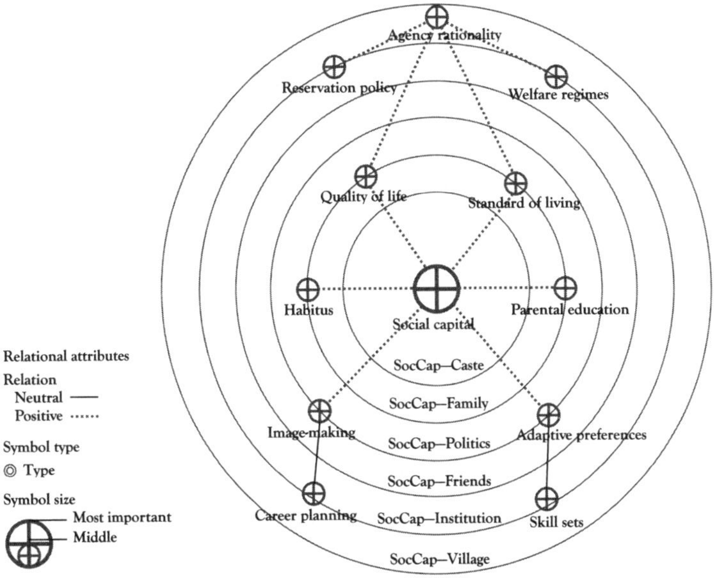

FIGURE 7.1 Social Capital: Network Map

Source: Created by the author.

where the erstwhile lower castes approach the reservation policy as state-sponsored social capital in India. However, the very same patronage polarises the 'others', and the consequence can be seen in the creation of an exclusivist social order.

Nevertheless, the welfare regime successfully addresses the caste-specific issues as 'protective' discrimination, and the erstwhile higher castes 'increasingly' withdraw themselves from everyday interaction orders. The result is invisible forms of social exclusion where the structure dictates the lives of the human agencies. These exclusive social processes can further be seen in terms of conversion factors.

According to the capabilities literature, the conversion factors represent how many functionings one can get out of a good or service. This, in the present context, is predominantly understood by the educated un/underemployed youths in Sripuram as corruption. As corruption is increasingly being 'rationalised', one can understand it in terms of the institutional dependencies of the human agencies in

Sripuram. The author's everyday observations and interactions with the youths during fieldwork confirm its centrality as a conversion factor, and they justify it as crucial to functionings formations. The author's attempts to understand the moral perspectives with which the youths viewed corruption were dismissed as 'idealistic talk'. Against this backdrop, one can depict the conversion factors as shown in Figure 7.2.

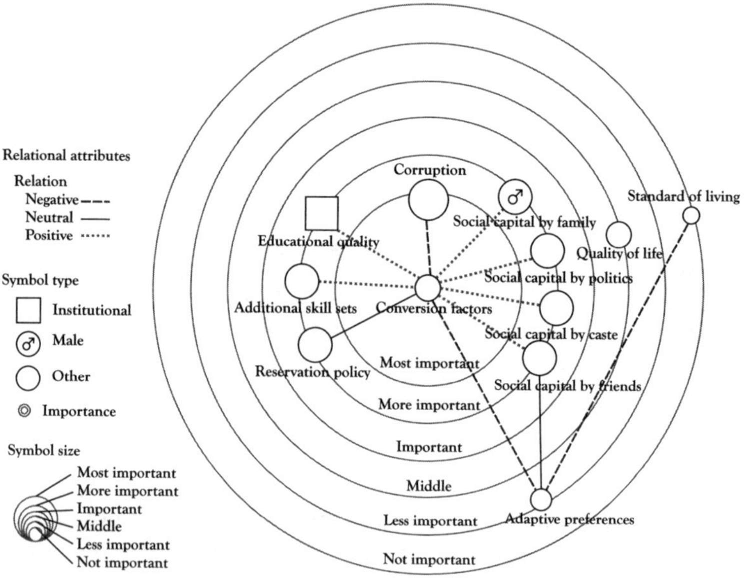

FIGURE 7.2 Conversion Factors: Network Map

Source: Created by the author.

There are numerous aspects which add to the complexities of these factors. These include institutional aspects like quality of education and family-based social capital. These factors must be described. For instance, family-based social capital is gendered where women are socio-economically subservient. The nature of economic 'determinism' most often shapes the social structure where gender is differentially institutionalised. Nevertheless, there are exceptions, as the erstwhile higher caste women are generally assertive due to education and employment, but their dependency on the male head of the family persists.

For this reason, social capital by family, caste and even politics plays a complex role, where patriarchy often gets re/produced. Also, the quality of education and reservation policy play significant roles in individuals' expansion of the avenues of mobility. The social processes of these options 'ensure' standard of living and quality of life. Though this could be a social re/production of inequalities, the poor people's subjectivities seemingly rationalise them within the systemic structures.

Social Reproduction

As education is a process of human socialisation, diverse groups shape it according to their structural locations. This is mostly complicated by intersectional dynamics. Due to this, the educational outcomes of the Pallars are increasingly low in contrast to the 'others'. Cultural habitus and social capital shape their functionings as intrinsically inferior to the hegemonic demands of the market. But the same system of education is successfully producing 'employable' individuals among 'others'. The caste system in/visibly plays its role where Brahmin youths with their social capital, at times, find it relatively easy to get a job in Chennai even if they have had a similar education like the others. The gender dimension runs almost parallel to this complexity: only very few women have been successful in shaping their educational functionings, with a 'natural' exception of those belonging to the upper castes.

The non-availability of economic resources and social opportunities convinces the Brahmins that emigration is the only option for economic mobility in Sripuram. However, the success of economic emigration to nearby towns and cities is further influenced by social capital. In this context, the immediate emigration is seemingly to the state capital, Chennai. Thus, the economic aspirations for mobility often drive the villagers out to where the role of social capital is significant. This is in sharp contrast to the 'others' in Sripuram. The extent of their skills mostly determines the employability of the Pallars. As could be expected, neither do they have adequate social capital due to historical reasons, nor can they enhance their innate abilities at present. The process of learning from education enhances one's abilities with functional skills and capabilities. However, given their inferior socio-economic positions, the Pallars must depend on the mediocre services of government schools, which fail to provide them with enabling conditions for capabilities or functionings formations. The result is the label of being 'educated' in the village without 'freedom'. Santhanam, a teacher at the local school, when enquired about the emigration patterns among the different castes, suggested that: 'The younger generation shall be educated well, but at the same time, they need to settle down in the village to uphold their caste traditions. Otherwise, the livelihood balance will be lost. Consequently, people may suffer' (interview from the field, dated 16 November 2011).

This correlates educational functionings as the status stabiliser of tradition. The structural interpretations of this nature define the complexities of emigration in Sripuram. Also, Bhairavi, an influential 'intellectual' in the village, argues that:

> Education-induced emigration creates nuclear families in society. This, in turn, produces households and individuals as islands in the urban anonymity. The result is even very close relatives cannot be entertained in these families. This is against our national tradition of having more extensive kinship networks. Therefore, the younger generation today do not have a higher level of social capital which we had from our family system. (Interview from the field, dated 12 November 2011.)

Considering these functionalist standpoints, educated youths with limited social opportunities and economic mobility are pushed out of the village. The unemployed Brahmins (whether educated or not) usually take up odd jobs like those of a cook or Purohit. In this, caste-based social capital readily assists them to be mobile. In contrast, non-Brahmins must find other economic avenues now that caste-based division of labour has been reduced. However, non-Brahmins do not have cultural capital; the state's reservation policy is generally viewed by the Brahmins and other high castes in terms of vote-bank politics.

Furthermore, the consequence of this can be seen in newer social formations along the lines of the endogamous unification of the castes to shake off the sect-wise differences. This 'self-adjustment' of the status quo has taken many forms. For instance, marital restrictions among the different Brahmin sects are no longer perceived to be relevant. Some of the present generation of Brahmins do not even know these differences. This is a significant change in Sripuram today, in contrast to the earlier descriptions of Béteille (1965a).

The role of education in this newer social formation is essential where modernisation 'democratises' institutions. For example, the role of the Archahars[16] was traditionally performed by Brahmins, who cannot naturally claim their ascribed status in temples today. The role allocation needs to have state approval, in which politics has the final say,[17] as demography determines the political economy of the state. The consequence is that the higher the caste, the lower the status in the political system.

Also, one must be aware that not all Brahmins are highly educated and economically prosperous.[18] An aged Brahmin villager, Narashimhan, for instance, asserted that 'the only developmental option available for the Madapalli Brhamanan is to catch the next train to Madras even without a valid ticket' (interview from the field, dated 16 November 2011).[19] Although there are a few such cases, Brahmins in general seem skilful 'enough' to survive the economic deprivation in the village. Here, the role of social capital and educational functionings plays an important part. However, the failures of Brahmin youths in the labour market put them in another kind of deprivation in personhood. If they cannot migrate to bigger cities like Chennai, they end up becoming Purohits or doing odd jobs in the village and nearby areas.

In consequence, most of them have not been able to find a match for marriage. As this is seemingly due to their 'higher' social status where the women are economically better placed, it constructs inferior personhood in the Agraharam. Brahmin girls are often advised by the elders 'to study further to get a good husband'. By contrast, the other castes do not face such demands because their preferences are focused on occupational outcome to retain primordial privileges. This is also seemingly due to them not having received quality education in the past.

Mainstream literature treats education as an automatic solution for all developmental ills. This human capital ideal shall not mislead the capitalist approach. It is therefore essential to understand the current framework of intersectional complexities when it comes to education. Caste is not a homogeneous entity: the threefold classification of the Sripuram society into Brahmins, OBCs and SCs highlights the complex heterogeneities where the recognition of social structure could be a way out in capabilities approach–specific studies in India. This has been highlighted by how the knowledge-centric lifestyles of the Brahmins, along with a turn towards modernity of the OBCs and the state's supportive political economy to the erstwhile backward castes are seemingly convincing diverse groups to come out of their orthodoxies. However, the adaptive preferences of their human agencies, along with changing structural reality have often been overlooked by mainstream academic narratives so far. The notions of capabilities are thus initiated from employment-centrism due to the intersectional dynamics of caste and class positions of the poor in India.

Even human agency does not see education as part of the broader notions of capabilities; nor does the employment-centric approach assure people of the economic possibilities out of it. The primary reason for this dichotomy is intersectional. This chapter has analysed the complexities of capabilities formation and the limitations of the capabilities approach in a collectivist social order. In this analysis, it has been established that although caste-based divisions of labour have increasingly been eliminated due to their dysfunctionalities, the state has failed to create any alternative social opportunities so far.

Consequently, it complicates the social construction of capabilities by the reproduction of inequalities in the newer forms of the structure—systemic and human agencies. Against this backdrop, this chapter has argued that the perspective of the capabilities approach can conceptualise how these spheres could decide the capabilities alternatives. This is important, as capabilities without 'normative' listing (Nussbaum 2011) could be an 'absolute' entitlement. Theoretical engagements between capitals and capabilities can enrich sociological contributions in developmental studies.

Notes

1. See, for instance, Jha (2005).
2. In contrast, Sen (1997: 1960) argues that despite the usefulness of the concept of human capital as a productive resource, 'it is important to see human beings in a broader perspective than that of human capital'.

3. Brahmaniyam is a colloquial term for priestly roles, mainly to perform rites and rituals. Brahmaniyam among the youths in Sripuram is often manifested in the role of the Kurukkal. Traditionally, the Kurukkals were supposed to belong to a particular sect of the Brahmins and study the rules of Ahamam in separate Vedic schools or Vedha Pathsalas (a kind of school system where one graduates to become a Kurukkal). A Kurukkal's way of life is mandated by both caste and religion. They professionally thrive by officiating Smartha temples. A Purohit, on the other hand, officiates the rituals in Smartha Brahmin households. The dilution of the roles of the Purohit and Kurukkal by Brahmin EUEYs underscores the newer forms of caste in the village.

4. For further details, see the Hindu Religious and Charitable Endowments Department website, available at https://tnhrce.gov.in/hrcehome/index.php (accessed 12 May 2011)

5. Pallar children in Sripuram skip school for various reasons, which include their disinterestedness in studies. This is seemingly due to their habitus, where numerous factors such as familial and social contexts render them uncertain of navigating the complexities of life.

6. Some of the youths in Sripuram call this 'street-smartness'.

7. Brahmothsavam is a typical Brahmin festival in both Vaishnava as well as Smartha temples.

8. Chennai, formerly known as Madras, is the capital of Tamil Nadu, which is one of the five southern states with a population of nearly 70 million people, as per the 2011 Census report.

9. See, for instance, Lipsky (1969).

10. See, for instance, Cleaver (2005), Coleman (1988) and Migheli (2011), among others.

11. Jackson (2005: 107) explains: 'Allowing for the social context of capabilities requires explicit recognition of social structures, both personal and impersonal, as some capabilities may be due to employment or other roles and membership of social networks.'

12. It must be noted that non-Brahmins (including the OBCs and Pallars) generally do not have any of these ceremonies apart from punniyajanam.

13. During fieldwork in 2012, the author found that the entire state of Tamil Nadu did not have a regular supply of electricity and water. For instance, electricity was available for only 15 hours a day or so. This is odd, considering the various official reports that claim Tamil Nadu to be one of the 'developed' states in India (Government of India 2011).

14. The presence of a nameplate is symbolic of the socio-economic credentials of the household.

15. It must be mentioned that in Sripuram, the local Brahmins generally represent the former, and the Pallars the latter.

16. Archahar is often called Kurukkal in Tamil. Though it primarily means the priest of the Smartha temple, in colloquial usage it denotes non-Brahmin priests in Tamil Nadu at present.

17. This is in line with the Hindu Religious and Charitable Endowments Department. For details, see https://tnhrce.gov.in/hrcehome/index.php (accessed 12 May 2011).

18. Driver (1982: 228) has established that caste and occupational hierarchy are no longer parallel to one another.

19. Madapalli Brahmins, colloquially, refer to economically poor Brahmins.

eight

Social Change in Sripuram

In Education Studies, the capabilities approach successfully offers a scholastic critique to the human capital approach. Contrary to powerful critiques showing the limitations of this approach (Nussbaum 2010; Robeyns 2006; among others), the present ethnographic research finds employment-centric instrumentalism prevalent in Sripuram. The central argument of the work highlights the social construction of capabilities in Sripuram. This underscores the complex interactions between individual agents in their caste–class positions where the thesis challenges the constitutive and intrinsic aspects of education with instrumentalist notions of the human capital approach.

Visits to the local school and orphanage in Sripuram as part of this ethnographic fieldwork have revealed that institutionalised welfare structures with poor learning outcomes are re/producing the deprivation trap in the village. Reflexive analyses from the fieldwork have further found that the well-being of the children is mostly based on their institutional presence and human agency in the social structure. The children, in turn, are deprived of the basics of life due to class and caste positions in the social structure as well as in the hierarchical stratifications of the village.[1] They are further marginalised due to the poor infrastructure of the orphanage and mediocre quality of education at the local school. Given these disadvantages, this analysis based on the social construction of capabilities concludes that neither the broad notions of capabilities nor the narrow views of functionings are proximate to the children's agential well-being in Sripuram.

Differential educational outcomes of the various social groups have been conceptualised taking into account their systemic segregations along socio-economic differences. As this segregation questions the notions of social justice in the country, it is important to note that the poor shall not be left alone in the government schools, which are notoriously of low quality. This is important because 'with adequate social opportunities, an individual can effectively shape their own destiny and help each other' (Sen 1999b: 11). One possible solution could be to increase the quality standards to make government schools attractive for all, including the non-poor. In addition to the discussion on deprivations suffered by the children, the central arguments of this book discuss functionings formations as well as the failures of the EUYs and EUEYs in Sripuram. The adaptive preferences and coping strategies of the educated un/underemployed youths in the informal economies of Meenakshipuram and Sripuram thus underline the social construction of capabilities. In this social construction, intersectionality of caste and class plays a complex role in education and employment. Against this backdrop, it is pertinent to discuss social change in Sripuram.[2]

Historically, changes in social institutions 'have been qualitative and divergent rather than cumulative and unidirectional ...' (Béteille 2009b: 98). In this context, the changes in Sripuram can broadly be understood in terms of caste as well as education. In this re-study of a classical sociological field site, Béteille's descriptions have provided the conceptual background for understanding the process of change. This has also allowed the present work to compare the descriptions. For instance, Béteillian descriptions of Sripuram as an Agraharam village or a Brahmin village are no longer the social reality today. The Brahmins leaving the village because of various socio-economic reasons and the immigration of the non-Brahmins inside the Agraharam provide a new flavour to these descriptions. It is appropriate to quote Fuller (2012) keeping in mind this newer reality:

> To this day, in Sripuram and other Brahmin villages in Tamilnadu, *Cheris* remain separated from the main village settlement areas and are exclusively inhabited by Dalits, but *Agraharams*, on the other hand, though still clearly demarcated, now have both Brahmin and Non-Brahmin residents, with the Brahmins often being in the minority, so that old rules restricting access have been abandoned. (Ibid.: *xxxii*)

The residential changes within Sripuram can further be explained by population and household figures of the village today. In order to understand this change, it is interesting to compare the present-day population with Béteille's 1960 description (Table 8.1).

TABLE 8.1 Social Change in Sripuram: Population, 1960 and 2010

Caste Group	*1960*	*2010*
Brahmins	341	210
Non-Brahmins	688	820
Adi-Dravida	371	460
Total	1,400	1,490

Note: The figures of the present research in the year 2010 have been contrasted with the figures of 1960 taken from Béteille (2012: 26).

Source: Created by the author.

Thus, the total population of all the communities presently living in Sripuram is around 1,500. This includes 460 Pallars or the SCs (183 adult males, 152 adult females, 65 male children and 60 female children); 820 OBCs including MBCs and BCs (350 adult males, 320 adult females, 80 male children and 70 female children); and 210 Brahmins (100 adult males, 90 adult females, 10 male children and 10 female children).

These figures are in sharp contrast to the population breakdown by caste group in 1960, as per Béteille's fieldwork in the village. One can observe a notable decline in both population as well as the number of Brahmin households (Table 8.2). In contrast, the other two segments, the non-Brahmins and the Pallars, have grown steadily over the years.

TABLE 8.2 Social Change in Sripuram: Households, 1960 and 2010

Caste Group	*1960*	*2010*
Brahmins	92	65
Non-Brahmins	168	209
Adi-Dravida	89	103
Total	349	377

Note: The 2010 figures have been collected by the present research and the 1960 figures are given in Béteille (2012: 26).

Source: Created by the author.

Although the total number of houses is relatively stable, with an increase in just 28 houses over five decades, there are a few salient points to be explained. Out of the total 209 non-Brahmin households in 2010, eight are Christian households. They occupy in a small street within the Kudiana or the non-Brahmin street. The OBCs households altogether (including the 25 'outsiders' who are living in the Agraharam) number around 234 today. In the Kudiana, there are around 13 unoccupied houses or empty flats. In addition, 17 houses remain unoccupied in the Agraharam. It is interesting that no such empty flats are available in the Pallar Cheri, which, as mentioned earlier, is still an exclusive residential unit of the Pallars.

The caste-based residential segregation is changing with a change in class positions in Sripuram. This can be seen in the increasing entry of non-Brahmins in the village. The settlement patterns in the Agraharam at present are no longer consistent with caste categorisations. The 25 OBC households in the Agraharam are increasingly secularising their conventional ways of living. Though these households represent the middle-class family structure, one can see them diluting the caste rigidities in the years to come. Also, the empty houses in the Agraharam are slowly being purchased by the non-Brahmins from outside Sripuram. Financially, some of them are richer in comparison to the local Brahmin residents. This further alters the living patterns whereby relationships become 'formalised' in the Agraharam. This is quite unusual according to the village standards. Against this backdrop, the competition for purchasing land is different for the diverse social groups in Sripuram. The Brahmins who are better educated than the others are generally interested in buying houses outside the village. The economic rationale is to purchase them as investment. The Pallars on the other hand are gradually competing to buy up the agricultural lands. Some of the OBCs who received lands from the Brahmin absentee landlords are gradually leaving the agricultural profession like the Brahmins. This symbolises the gradual agentic exodus from agriculture, where the role of education in the village is influential.

Caste and Change

The nature and form of the caste system in Sripuram are no longer the same as in the earlier 1960 study. This could be due to the political economy of the anti-Brahmin movements in Tamil Nadu. Though these movements have practically abolished Brahminism as a dominant ideological frame, they have given birth to Dravidian politics (based on non-Brahmin identities) at present. Although there is a widespread societal change, caste remains important as a form of primordial identity. These identities are generally not explicit in Tanjore town due to urban anonymity, but they are still visible in the everyday lives in villages like Sripuram, where, for instance, caste is tied to social capital. The result is a newer form of caste where '... it is becoming less and less meaningful to speak of the caste system as a rigid, hierarchical, tightly linked socioeconomic system' (Mencher 1970: 197).

Considering this changing reality, the higher levels of social distance among caste groups hold symbolic importance in interactions in the village. This is 'naturally' respected by the older generations, although the present-day youths are no longer bothered about it. This is seemingly due to the agential assertiveness of the present generations to exercise their identity and to 'question' the status quo. This is also happening among Brahmin youths who are increasingly secular in their outlook. This is mainly because of the broader political economy where the role of education is important. This is in contrast to Béteille's description—the present-day Brahmins are relatively sensitive to the others caste groups, which constitute a significant proportion of the population of Tamil Nadu. The cultural relativist reality is parallel to the newer identity formations of the Pallars in Sripuram. In addition to this, the political dynamics often secularise the caste groups in the demographic structure. However, despite the other positive changes, one still finds the prevalence of endogamy. When it comes to marital rules, caste as a social system predominates the lives of the villagers. This is in sharp contrast to urban locations like Chennai where one can see the growing incidents of marriages outside one's caste today.

Further, one can even observe changes in the nomenclature over the years. For instance, the Kudiana, or the street where the non-Brahmins or the OBCs live, is no longer a single residential unit. It has been converted into various streets. The way in which one identifies another caste by its name has also changed due to the broadening of the political economy. Before 1960, the present-day Dalits, for instance, were mostly addressed as Pallan in Sripuram. In the political structure of Béteille's period, it changed to Palla. Today it is Pallar. This marks a progressive and respectful naming of the caste group. Anyone who uses the earlier nomenclature of Pallan can be legally challenged (Devakumar 2017).

Furthermore, each caste has its traditional dressing pattern where one can find distinctive styles of clothing. On a typical day all groups wear similar clothes, but special occasions and festival days highlight the culture-specific differences in dress. The historical importance of Sanskrit as a cultural-religious language of the Brahmins has also been disappearing. The subtler aspects like 'purity norms' of food are changing. As long as the food is vegetarian, most Brahmins, with the exception of orthodox men, dine at the weddings of other caste groups.

Education and Social Change

As education is one of the primary forces for an individual's economic mobility, it is essential to understand its role in social change. Due to various socio-economic factors, Sripuram is losing its rural character. Education is one such factor. Although the changing socio-economic relationships within the village can be attributed to education, this aspect is overlooked in mainstream narratives. The changes in population as well as the number of households over the years have indicated the patterns of both mobility and migration of the social groups. The changes in the Agraharam, for instance, are mostly due to education-induced emigration of the Brahmins to larger cities. By comparison, the other segments of the population have moved only to informal economies like Meenakshipuram. Also, the differential educational outcome has reinforced the status quo where economic and social mobility of the individuals has confirmed the hierarchical nature of the social structure. However, the present-day Pallar youths who are educated, for instance, provide their caste group with a new reality in the village. This is important from the perspective of the capabilities approach: 'Non-farm jobs, better-paid wage labour and landowning, as well as education, have enabled a modicum of economic independence and changed the position of Dalits in the village. While change may not have led to employment, it heightened Dalits [*sic.*] sense of entitlement and confidence in relation to their erstwhile superiors' (Still 2011: 1124).

However, shrinking employment possibilities as well as the aversion of educated youths towards manual labour have pushed them out of the village. Due to this, one can mostly see the older generations residing in Sripuram. Also, as mentioned earlier, the number of Brahmin residents has decreased since 1960. It may not be surprising to see Sripuram without any Brahmin households in the next three or four decades. The increasing emigration of the educated youths to nearby towns clearly shows that education is an active agent that has urbanised the villagers in Sripuram. Though the absence of opportunities in the village is the oft-cited reason for the move, the role of education is the primary factor.

The decrease in the Brahmin population has not only changed the ways of life in the village, but has also altered the flavour of Sripuram. Their patronage of the local temples, for instance, is no longer taken as seriously as it was earlier. The composition of the students at the local school has changed as well. Béteille (2009a: 54) reported, 'As more and more Adi-Dravida children go to school and come into contact with both Non-Brahmin boys and girls, differences in speech tend to be leveled out, at least to some extent.' This is true even today due to the inter-mixing of the various castes at the local school. However, class differences still persist due to the non-poor people transferring to private institutions in Meenakshipuram. This re/produces a new gap in the social hierarchy based on the economic positions of the villagers.

Furthermore, the division of labour in the village is not merely an economic arrangement, but is also dependant on an inheritance-based social structure. Though the increasing levels of education are changing the landscape of this ascriptive status, the generational disadvantages of the Pallars do not allow them to break the cycle of economic deprivation and social exclusion. The role of social capital once again plays a differential role in preserving the status quo. However, '... the educated as well as the urban-employed have brought into the village secular values from the outside world. Such slight changes as could be noticed with regard to the relaxation of the ritual practices of pollution-purity rules were consequences of these new elements ...' (Ishwaran 1970b: 193).

These changes are crucial and sociologically significant. According to Béteille, 'In a field such as education, the demands of policy are important and urgent. But research directed solely by the requirements of policy tends to lose sight of the long-term changes taking place in a society' (quoted in Govinda 2011: *xvii*).

Notes

1. Related to this, see Harriss-White and Subramanian (1999) on 'illfare' in India.

2. A detailed discussion on social change in India can be seen, for instance, in Beals (1964, 1970); Davenport (1964); Gray (1965); Ishwaran (1970a); Kumar (1987); Mangalam (1965); Mencher (1970); Rolnick (1965); Sengupta (2008); Sivertsen (1963), among others.

nine

Conclusion

This book has approached the conception of capabilities not as personal traits of a human agency, but has located them within the framework of *social* construction. In this sense, capabilities are largely shaped by a complex set of factors. As everyone does not have the same *life chances* and *market situations*, there are differences in capabilities and functioning formations. The present work has critiqued the individualist traditions by underscoring the differences in terms of how agencies negotiate structures and systems. This is unique to a collective social order where individuals' agencies are negotiated across a broader *life-world*. This includes the intersectionality of caste, class and gender, among others. The present framework underlines the social complexities of capabilities formations while appreciating the non commensurability aspects (Sen 2009: 240).

The framework of the social construction of capabilities underscores the un/intended consequences of diverse identities negotiated across collective orders like that of the village in context; patriarchal structures stratified along caste and class dimensions; or educated youths' vulnerabilities in search of employment because of family constraints. The consequence goes beyond not only the structure–agency dualism, but also individualist and institutionalist positions.

Theoretical discourse emerging out of the empirical lives in Sripuram highlights that diverse contexts are influential not only in offering the enabling and disabling conditions, but also the conversion factors. The *systemic* conversion factors are exacerbated by unpredictable influences of the political economy. The ability to navigate structures and systems is complex, but there is a necessity to recognise the subtler nuances in lives. For instance, although the SCs and STs are conceived of as socio-economically backward groups, one can see marginalised individuals in every caste. This marginalisation among the higher castes could mostly be economic in nature. The result of an interplay among the various factors discussed in this book elucidates the complex social realities in a village like Sripuram. The disaggregation features of this complexity have been observed in the intersections. The cumulative effects of the socio-economic factors have set the ethnographic basis for adopting intersectional analyses. This has successfully allowed the social construction of capabilities framework to look at the issues in totality, instead of being carried away by 'empirical' reductionism. This is critical, as the quality of opportunities is determined to a large extent by a complex combination of factors which are predominantly shaped by diverse identities in India.

While the intersectional analysis is important, *social mobility can no longer be viewed as a movement of individuals from the ascriptive considerations of caste alone.* The subtleties of factors and availability of resources in socialising the next generation urgently need to be researched. This urgency must be observed regarding the role of intersectionality in reinforcing the influence of caste and class on recruitments *even* in the informal village economies. Also, it must be noted that the inequalities of opportunities that prevail among the erstwhile 'lower' castes are mostly due to their historical exclusion in society. As this has been well-established in academia (Breman 2004; Gorringe, Jeffrey and Sariola 2009, among others), the present framework argues that it is high time that the evolving complexities of the poor and the marginalised be underscored. The need of the hour is to study the mobility trajectories of the 'upper' stratum in the country. As this is critical for broader theory-building, it could also be a possible research lead for future capabilitarian studies.

Theorisation, it must be reiterated, is one of the important mandates of academia. Sociologists need to theorise the poor and the marginalised people in India differently, by countering economic determinism. For instance, if qualitative studies take up the issue of intersectional employment of the parents, it could add value at the conceptual level. This will allow academia to theorise the matrices of mobility. The sociological as well as ethnographic research, for instance, can contribute to the inter-generational mobility by sustained field observations. This is conceptually critical given statistical limitations. It is astonishing that even the NSS is under-sampling the rich. As this is also visible in mainstream academia, the consequence is that the measures understate the actual degree of inequality of income in India (Weisskopf 2011: 45). Thus, research that studies how the higher castes are navigating status will show how individual agencies are being shaped by intersectional forces in India today. In this backdrop, another probable research lead could be to understand how the non-poor people, mostly the erstwhile 'higher' castes, cultivate their children's talents and abilities. This is important, as it has functional conversion factors for broader capabilities and functioning formations (Sen 1999b). An analysis of this nature will also lead us to understand micro as well as macro social processes through which the family of one's origin re/produces well-being. This is important, as mainstream research has so far been unable to counter certain inconvenient truths in India.

Against this backdrop, the social construction of capabilities framework is significant, where the evaluative spaces of the capabilities approach have been located at the intersections of (economic) deprivations and (social) exclusions in Sripuram. In consequence, the comparative perspective has contrasted the marginal men with the 'others' in deconstructing the socio-economic mobilities. The central analyses, for instance, found *the irrelevance of landownership as a central criterion for identifying the poor in the village today*. In addition, it established the fact that neither class nor caste can exclusively constitute a community in the future. *It is the intersection of diverse societal factors that could play a definite role in the village.* Relatedly, the present work has portrayed the complexities of inequalities reproduced through differential outcomes in both functionings formations and capabilities. This underscores that the youths' educational 'successes' have neither ensured them broader notions of capabilities nor the skill to compete in the employment market. While the OBCs view this as a systemic collapse, the Brahmins view the same as agentic failure.

A survey of the literature brings forth that the analyses of employability and capabilities are under-researched in Indian education. In addition to filling this vacuum, this book revisits a Béteillean field-site to theoretically engage with Sen's capabilities approach. Towards this, the framework has deconstructed the complexities of capabilities and functionings formations. The effort to break the cycle of unemployability, for instance, differs across diverse caste groups. The institutional failures along with intersectional factors have reinforced the status quo in newer forms of inequality. Thus, the systemic inadequacies and structural exclusions cumulatively deprive the poor of functionings formations while also ensuring capabilities deprivations. The role of education with its differential outcomes across functionings and capabilities reinforces a newer vicious trap. The descriptions of the orphan children and educated youths have furthermore brought forth the complexities embedded across the unforeseen factors of life. This is important, as there is no single factor that is systemic, agentic or even structural in nature. It is the unpredictable combination of all these factors in relation to the complexities of life which plays an influential role in forming the elusive ideal called 'capabilities'.

The mainstream discourse, it must be noted, treats education as a pill for all developmental ills (Becker 1962, 1964; Becker and Tomes 1986; Gilead 2009; Schultz 1961, 1962; Sweetland 1996, among others). This human capital ideal should not mislead the capabilities approach. It is therefore essential to understand the complexity framework when it comes to education. Caste is not a homogeneous entity: the threefold classification of the Sripuram society into Brahmins, OBCs and SCs highlights the diverse heterogeneities where the recognition of social complexities could be a way out in capabilities studies in India. This has been highlighted by the knowledge-centric lifestyles of the Brahmins along with a turn towards modernity of the OBCs; the state's supportive political economy towards the erstwhile backward castes has further convinced diverse groups to come out of their orthodoxies. However, the adaptive preferences of their human agencies, along with changing structural reality, have often been overlooked by mainstream academic narratives so far. The notions of capabilities have thus insisted on the social complexities due to the fact that *even* the human agency does not see education as part of the broader notions of capabilities; nor does the employment-centric approach assure people of the economic possibilities out of it. The primary reason for this dichotomy is naturally intricate.

This establishes the fact that caste and capabilities are not parallel to one another, except in a few cases. Though caste as an endogamous unit provides a social capital base, the success or failure of the agencies in human capital is often intersected by systemic and structural interactions. Thus, the social re/production of inequalities often reinforces the existing arrangements in new forms. This can be seen in terms of the coping strategies of the poor, ranging from the way they adapt their preferences, or those enabling conditions which promise them the necessary conversion factors for functioning formations. This book has recognised the theoretical nuances of how the state has also been creating newer forms of inequalities by addressing historical hierarchies and disadvantages. As these opportunities and inequalities are embedded in the structures, systems and human agencies, one may consider this framework to be the search for a just society.

Appendix I

A Note on the Framework

In this note, the intention is to set the conceptual background for the thesis on the social construction of capabilities. Since the nineteenth century, the discipline of Development Studies has traversed various paradigms. This includes the human capital approach (HCA), followed by the basic needs apprach, entitlements approach, the human development school, and lastly, the capabilities approach. Analyses of these prominent theories of development provide the conceptual framework for highlighting the relevance of the capabilites approach at present.

Human Capital Approach

The underlying assumptions of the HCA lie in its conception of human beings as the *agents* of wealth producers.[1] The central proponents of the approach, T. W. Schultz (the 1979 Economics Nobel laureate) and Gary S. Becker (the 1992 Economics Nobel laureate), regarded human abilities mainly as economic utilities. Consequently, education and skills were considered to be forms of capital. Thus, HCA treats education predominantly as creating productive abilities for economic growth. As an economic paradigm, the analysis of the HCA is firmly based on the trickle-down approach in Development Studies. The assumption of trickle-down believed that the accumulation of wealth by the rich is good for the poor since some of the increased wealth of the rich 'automatically' percolates to the poor.

For this reason, most of the research methods are analysed on the primacy of (i) the rate of returns (RoR) approach and (ii) cost-benefit analyses (CBA) in education.[2] This economic determinism has, however, failed to articulate the questions of why there is un/underemployment even among the educated. This is critical in light of the constant emphasis on investment in education for the ideals of human capital formations. Also, the HCA is inadequate in answering the reasons for the decline in the standard of living despite the increased levels of educational attainment in society. As these concerns are significant, the current analysis takes them up in its central analyses. This is particularly relevant in the case of India where the conception of education under the Ministry of Human Resource Development is seemingly reduced to skill development along the lines of the human capital ideals.[3]

Basic Needs Approach

The basic needs approach was propounded by Paul Streeten, Frances Stewart, Shahid Javed Burki, Norman L. Hicks and Mahbub ul Haq, among others. The central assumption of this approach is based on the critique of HCA in Development Studies. The main concern has been rapid growth without substantial poverty reduction, generally due to the failure of the trickle-down method of HCA.[4] For instance, Streeten and Burki (1978: 411) have argued that the '... aggregate economic growth appears to have done very little for the poorer half of the Third World's rapidly growing populations'. As economic growth alone is not sufficient to improve the conditions of life of the poor substantially, they suggest the basic-needs bundles. This bundle consists of education, health, nutrition, water, sanitation and shelter for individuals and society to survive across the globe. In their view, prerequisites of these bundles are necessary due to '... the failure of growth of GNP to eliminate poverty which led to the new emphasis on basic needs' (Stewart 1980: 10). Though the approach underlines the basic minimum factors, some of the arguments give the impression that it is an extension of HCA. For instance, according to Hicks (1980: 23), the '... expenditure on basic needs improve the productivity of human resources, and can, therefore, be considered a form of long-term investment in human capital'. Also, other theorists hold a similar notion. To Wheeler (1980: 436), for instance, the '... improvements in health, nutrition, and education have labour augmenting productivity effects, so that basic needs expenditures strongly complement capital accumulation in the development process'. Thus, scholars over the years have discarded this approach merely as misguided welfare due to the obvious limitations of economic determinism.[5]

Entitlements Approach

In his research on poverty and famines, Amartya Sen advocated the entitlements approach. The central assumption of this approach questions the Malthusian theory (that food supply falls relative to the size of the population). As Sen has identified the limitations of food availability decline, his analyses are based on three crucial assumptions.[6] The first is that famines depend not *merely* on production, but also on distribution (Sen 1976: 1273). This is followed by the assertion that famines can take place even without substantial food availability decline (Sen 1981: 459). Moreover, famines can be analysed as 'failures of entitlement relations'. Based on these assumptions, he investigated famines by focusing on variations on endowments and exchange entitlements mappings. This is what he calls the entitlements approach.

Thus, Sen has redefined welfare economics by proving that starvation '... is a matter of some people not *having* enough food to eat, and not a matter of there *being* not enough food to eat' (ibid.: 434). This disproved the Malthusian approach to famine. In his view (Sen 1986), the entitlement-set of a person 'is determined by his original bundle of ownership (what is called his "endowment" and the various alternative bundles he can acquire starting respectively from each initial endowment, through the use of trade and production (what is called his "exchange entitlement mapping")'. These conceptual categories, as we will see later, set the background for his future contributions in Development Studies. The contributions of the entitlements approach specifically set the context for the current development paradigm, the capabilities approach. If a person, to quote Sen (1980: 616), 'has not got enough food, this can be *either* because he did not have the *ability* to command that food, or because he *chose* not to exercise that ability'. The approach, like other mainstream thoughts in Development Studies, has however been 'appropriated' by the economic determinism. Sen (1987: 31) acknowledges it as: 'the problem of world hunger is not purely economic one, even though the economic issues are of major importance and call for an adequately deep investigation. Even, the notion of entitlement which has obvious economic content, cannot escape having legal connotations, political implications and *social* relevance' (emphasis added).

Human Development School

The human development (HD) school is a conceptual extension of earlier developmental thoughts. This school is propounded mainly by Mahbub ul Haq and Amartya Sen. Their work has been additionally supported by other research.[7] According to this school, human development is a process of 'enlarging' people's *choices*. This is accomplished most fundamentally by living a long and healthy life, being educated, and having a decent standard of living. For the measurement, Haq and Sen created an index called the human development index (HDI). It 'is the equally weighted sum of deprivation of a country with respect to each of three components: life expectancy at birth, literacy, and real income per head' (Srinivasan 1994: 238).

Like other earlier approaches, the human development school is also critical of the trickle-down effects and economic determinism. For instance, it criticises previous paradigms regarding (i) the growth failures in poverty eliminations over the years; and (ii) the inadequacy of gross national product (GNP) as a measure of human well-being. These two concerns have been well articulated in the literature. For instance, McGillivray (1991: 1461) has argued that the '... development levels ought not to be assessed by income measures alone and that one must take into account *social* and human welfare criteria' (emphasis added). Also, Hopkins (1991: 1469) established how '... the poverty of the people in many countries of the developing world has been no barrier to the affluence of their armies'.

In contrast to the basic needs bundles, the human development school holds three critical variables (namely longevity, knowledge and living standards). However, its index has also been criticised by various researchers. For instance, Streeten has questioned the relevance of HDI. To him, '... the concept of human development is much deeper and richer than what can be caught in any index or set of indicators'. So, 'why try to catch a vector in a single number?' (Streeten 1994: 235). Among other critics, Srinivasan (1994: 240) was vocal in his argumentation. For him, the components of HDI, namely life expectancy and educational attainment, are 'functionings' in Sen's sense, but their *relative* values need not be the same across individuals, countries and socio-economic groups (ibid.). Thus, these critical engagements require Development Studies to accommodate the critiques into a newer paradigm. Against this backdrop, Sen's unconsolidated writings have been incorporated into a paradigm of the capabilities approach.

Capabilities Approach

The capabilities approach is predominantly based on the works of Sen and Nussbaum.[8] Though Sen is the founding figure, Nussbaum has extended it as the theory of social justice. The central tenets of the approach hold two critical concepts: capabilities and functionings. It is appropriate to define them here. Whereas capabilities are substantive freedom, functionings are the achieved outcomes. These two concepts are thus evaluative spaces of the approach. These spaces firmly hold the framework that the notion of development is a process of expanding real freedoms. It means that the real purpose of development is to enlarge people's choices in all fields—social, economic and political dimensions. Accordingly, individual or agential aspects of development become the central concern.

As a logical extension to the human development school, the relation between the capabilities approach and human development is differentially understood in the literature. Some view the capabilities approach as providing a theoretical foundation for human development (Robeyns 2005: 94), while others analyse it as a smaller input to the more critical approach of human development (Gasper 2007: 357). Although the approach holds many promising concepts, it nevertheless has critics. For instance, Jackson (2005: 105), whose critique sets the background for the present work, points out that 'the social context of capabilities has been latent in Sen's work but marginal and under-theorised'. This limitation, by not addressing the importance of social structure, makes neither the capabilities approach as successful in its operationalisation, nor shuns its 'individualistic' tag so far. Also, Robeyns (2005: 110) has argued that 'the disciplinary terrains are so far under-explored'.

The present book, considering the concerns, attempts to explore the social construction of capabilities in Sripuram. As sociological research, the central analysis explores the role of social structure in educational functionings of the poor in Sripuram. Thus, the research holds the capabilities approach as a conceptual framework for its analyses. Also, theoretical implications of the thoughts on development have been incorporated into the relevant aspects of the analyses. Though these theoretical paradigms have given a conceptual grounding to education over the years, there are two central concerns. One is their consistent opposition to economic determinism, which is followed by their concern for distributive justice in society. The brief survey in this note, however, highlights the historical failures. First, distributive justice has been an elusive goal over the years. Though this elusiveness is setting developmental failures across the globe, one cannot find reason for economic determinism. It seems that this is mainly due to the limited sociological presence as well as the mainstream positivist ideals in the social sciences at present (Venkataraman 2016b).

These two central concerns, therefore, highlight the necessity of addressing distributive justice by conceptually avoiding economic determinism. The present book attempts to address them by appreciating the intersectional social reality. This reality is critical as it is further complicated by a neo-liberal political economy, which privileges the importance of the market in its developmental paradigm. Considering this paradigm, one must conceive the fact that the nature of a state and its withdrawal from public policy commitments in development differ across countries. The 'withdrawal' of the state in the First World, for instance, is comparatively tolerable due to the 'near-perfect' nature of the social welfare systems and well-developed social infrastructure. This is in sharp contrast to the Third World where countries like India have a persistent macro-economic pressure to 'open-up' the economy without adequately ensuring social welfare: for instance, the absence of social insurance regarding unemployment allowance and quality medical assistance at the time of emergency. The result is the elite re/production of social order where the poor are the worst sufferers. Their everyday encounters with the state are often asymmetrical.[9] The result is the strengthening of different socio-economic structures in the country. In this developmental complication, the role of education becomes critical due to its promising 'dynamic' ideals.

It is pertinent to sociologically focus on educational functionings of the poor to highlight the importance of social structure in the analysis of capabilities formations. Thus, the present research has aimed at primarily addressing the concerns of Jackson (2005: 105), as outlined earlier.

NOTES

1. See, for instance, Becker (1962, 1964); Becker and Tomes (1986); Gilead (2009); Schultz (1961, 1962); and Sweetland (1996), among others.

2. See, for instance, Becker (1962, 1964) and Schultz (1961, 1962), among others.

3. For similar arguments, see, for instance, Venkataraman (2016a).

4. See, for instance, Hicks (1980); Hicks and Streeten (1979); Reader (2006); Stewart (1980); Streeten (1971); Streeten and Burki (1978); and Wheeler (1980), among others.

5. As mentioned in Wheeler (1980: 435).

6. See, for instance, Sen (1976, 1981, 1986, 1987).

7. See, for instance, Apthorpe (1997); Aturupane, Glewwe and Isenman (1994); Desai (1991); Fukuda-Parr (2003, 2011); Fukuda-Parr and Kumar (2003); Gasper (2002); Haq (2003); Hopkins (1991); Kelley (1991); Lind (1992); McGillivray (1991); Mehrotra (2005); Nussbaum (2011); Rampal (2000); Sen (2000); Srinivasan (1994); Streeten (1994); and Trabold-Nübler (1991), among others.

8. See also, for instance, Dean (2009); Deneulin and McGregor (2010); Fukuda-Parr (2003, 2011); Gasper (2002, 2007); George (2010); Jackson (2005); Levine (2004); Migheli (2011); Nussbaum (2006, 2011); Reader (2006); Robeyns (2000, 2005, 2006); Saith (2001); Sen (1997, 1999a, 1999b, 2004); and Zimmermann (2006), among others. In addition, the capability perspective has been extended to education research by Otto and Ziegler (2013); Saito (2003); Unterhalter (2003a, 2003b); Walker (2006); and Walker and Unterhalter (2007).

9. For similar arguments, see, for instance, Corbridge et al. (2005) and Venkataraman (2018c).

Appendix II

Reflections on the Method

To understand the educational functionings of the poor with the intention of deconstructing the social construction of capabilities, the evaluative spaces of the capabilities approach have been conceptualised intersectionally. Given the fact that ethnographic work '... is an exercise in "thick description", trying to interpret meaning regarding what people understand, think about, and how they describe their behaviour' (Geertz 1973),[1] the present work has adopted it as a research method. This is understandable because ethnography '... is both a method (data collection technique) and a methodology (a theoretical and philosophical framework)' (Brewer 1994: 231).[2]

Ethnography as a written account primarily focuses on a community and analytically describes its way of life and institutions in a given society. In Berreman's (2011: 156) definition, it is '... a written report summarising the behaviours, and the beliefs, understandings attitudes, and values they imply, of a group of interacting people'. In this context, the present framework employs it for data collection and interpretation. While observation is the primary research tool to document the oral accounts of the respondents, qualitative follow-ups have also been employed. This includes the everyday interactions in the field and telephonic follow-up discussions during the study period.

For an in-depth qualitative understanding, the author has conducted ethnographic fieldwork in Sripuram. Observational aspects of the fieldwork were supported by semi-structured interviews to study the meanings and interpretations of educational outcomes within poor households in their cultural settings.[3] For documenting thick ethnographic descriptions, the observation method has been used for primary sources of data collection. To understand the macro-structures, the author also made use of the relevant academic literature as well as policy documents on the subject. This has helped to conceptually understand the context of capabilities and functionings formations through issues of education quality and employability. Subsequently, the author engaged with diverse social groups during the data collection period in the village.

The selection of the village was based on its social stratification system and its composition of diverse groups. Data collection and analyses have thus been primarily based on reflexive field notes. This has been accompanied by handling of available sources of information on the subject. This includes the author's visit to the nearby towns of Sripuram in addition to living in the village during the fieldwork periods. The author visited the district as well as state headquarters to collect secondary sources of information to substantiate the central arguments. Furthermore, the author consulted libraries[4] both in Tamil Nadu and New Delhi during different phases of the study.

The Conceptual Factors

In India, the socially marginalised members, namely the SCs, suffer both exclusion and economic deprivation. Since this study aims at a subjective definition of research categories, the choice of method has naturally been ethnographic. Hence, economic deprivation has been conceptualised in terms of the theory of relative deprivation.[5] In this process, exclusion is understood mainly from sociological perspectives.

It must be mentioned in this context that learning outcomes of the marginalised section are meagre in India. This is due to various structural as well as systemic factors. The current research attempts to understand both these factors in capabilities as well as functioning formations of the poor in Sripuram. Since analysis of this kind is due in the country, attempts have been made to document the complex social realities involved in the educational outcomes. Thus, a conceptual analysis of functionings can be a guiding force to identify the analytical categories. At the theoretical level, the capabilities approach has navigated the arguments of educational functionings in Sripuram.

The Approach

Ethnography is a qualitative approach to study the cultural patterns and perspectives of people in their natural settings. The central assumption has succinctly been documented by Hammersley (1990):

> ... the nature of social world must be *discovered*; that this can only be achieved by first-hand observation and participation in "natural" settings, guided by an exploratory orientation; that accounts of the findings of such research must capture the processes involved and the social meanings that generate them. On the basis of these assumptions, ethnography is directed towards producing what are referred to as "theoretical", "analytical" or "thick" descriptions (whether of societies, small communities, organizations, spatial locations, or social world). These descriptions must remain close to the concrete reality of particular events but at the same time reveal general features of human social life. (Ibid.: 598)

Thus, it must be mentioned that ethnography is methodologically 'trying to interpret meaning regarding what people understand, think about, and how they describe their behaviour' (Geertz 1973). This is in contrast to methodologies of positivistic frameworks where the importance of scientific 'objectivity' is stressed. Against these two extreme methodological positions, there are approaches which blend both as a mixture of methods and triangulation in research. But, given the nature of the present enquiry, the importance of ethnography '... lies in its depth penetration of a topic or area, it yields explanatory insights into the reasons why people, groups, and organizations act as they do, and how conflicting social forces are resolved' (Adler and Adler 1987: 17). As ethnographic research trends have already '... stormed the ivory tower and have become more central to academic knowledge production at the end of the twentieth century than ever before' (Anderson 1999: 452), the current research believes in its radical potential. This provides the methodological tools to understand the subjective definitions of poverty and other chosen analytical schemes. While the purpose of this study is to describe, analyse and interpret educational outcomes, an attempt has been made to research larger theoretical frameworks of the capabilities approach. Also, given the fact that these subjective endeavours 'cannot easily capture in interviews and quantified information' (Madan 1998), the study has followed the research processes described in the next section.

Research Processes

The focus has primarily been on systematic observations, and qualitative descriptions of the poor have been supported by field notes and interview transcripts. The present work considers this method as close to reality as data produced by structured interviews or questionnaires. To capture the field in all its 'naturalness' (Stoddart 1986: 108), both observation and semi-structured interviews have been conducted. The observation of the daily routines of the villagers and their in-depth analyses have yielded rich qualitative inputs for the research.

Moreover, by attending every possible community gathering, informal dialogues have also been initiated with the educated un/underemployed youths, children, teachers, community leaders and parents of the economically poorer households in the village. The observation has primarily been based on the process of *disattending* to understand the educational outcomes of the poor. The observations of the author in this process are guided by the notion of invisibility in the field: 'The invisible researcher is the ideal researcher who sees without being observed and, consequently, captures the natural field without tainting it' (ibid.: 108–09).

Hence, for documenting the oral accounts of the villagers, qualitative follow-ups have also been done. As contextualised exercises enable profound understanding, the author constructs a conceptual mapping of the village. Besides, the author also built a profile of the community. The documented oral accounts out of ethnographic data collection processes have been transcribed with the assistance of software (f4) in developing reflexive insights. The analysis has further been assisted by qualitative software packages like Atlas Ti and VennMaker.

APPENDIX II.1 Ethnographic Focus[6]

Categories	*Respondents*
Educational outcomes of the poor [functionings]	EUEYs, EUYs and orphan children
Capabilities acquired [through education]	
Social capital	EUEYs, EUYs, orphan children, teachers and opinion leaders

Source: Author's fieldwork.

For observation, field visits were planned along the Malinowskian dictum of *immersion-detachment-immersion*.[7] Also, if the field area is one's society, as in the case of the present work, Srivastava's (2004: 19) suggestion has been taken care of: '... [T]he field happens to be easily accessible and ... they can always go back to the field for a couple of weeks in the midst of writing up their work.' Furthermore, to theorise upon the observed reality, the author also attempted to take Adler and Adler's (1987: 9) suggestion of 'withdrawing some months and returning for another extended period ...'. Against this backdrop, the author conducted fieldwork in several phases since 2008.[8] Different phases of the fieldwork were supported by regular discussions and consultations for the study. In the end, it must be stated that the research methods such as participant observation and semi-structured interviewing are '... in need of greater exploration' (ibid.: 6), in India. Though these may not the answer all questions, they '... can address some issues better than any other approach' (Adler and Adler 1995: 27). This is critical, considering the mainstream positivist research trends in the country.[9]

THE NATIVE FACTORS

Regarding methodology, the author reflected upon some aspects of cultural relativism. Given the ethnographic attempt to document the social construction of capabilities, nativity plays an important role. As 'imperfect knowledge of the language introduces limitations to the research' (Berreman 2011: 184), the present work has natural advantages in the field due to the author's linguistic abilities as a native speaker. This has allowed him to understand the respondents' perspectives directly instead of merely relying on the version of the local informants. This is advantageous as: 'If the ethnographer cannot understand any of the conversations between interpreter and the informant, he is completely at the mercy of the interpreter; what he learns is filtered and inevitably interpreted, and to an extent, distorted before he hears it' (ibid.: 185).

Srinivas also acknowledges the natural factors through language proficiency. Thus, regarding language, the 'gate-keeping' factors have been controlled in this work. This has allowed the author to grasp the intricacies of everyday social realities of the village. The present study is set in a district in Tamil Nadu different to the one to which the author belongs. While there is a difference between the knowledge of the investigator acquired by virtue of their being a natural member of society and the one they acquire by consciously undertaking its study (Srivastava 2004: 22), this has helped maintain value-neutrality in the research. Also, the author, though a Tamil Nadu native, has not lived in the state since 2003.

Advantages of Studying One's Own Society

Apart from linguistic advantages discussed earlier, there are other rewards when one studies one's own society. For instance, if the researcher keeps their criticality open, they have the benefit of going beyond the expected portrayal of a society. An outsider will painfully take time to understand the society and its dynamic setting. The native researcher can utilise this period to scrutinise the factors which operate beyond the surface. For this, the native researcher has a definite advantage over an outsider. This has methodologically helped the author as well.

There is a further advantage when the '... insider who takes up the posture of an outsider, by his training as an anthropologist or a sociologist and looks at his own culture, hoping to be surprised. If he is, only then may he achieve new understandings' (Madan 1975: 149).[10] This fresh understanding with a 'depth of the involvement of the insider in his society is likely to invest his work with relevance and urgency which the outsider work is not likely to possess' (Srinivas 2004:

419). Although ethnography or even to an extent qualitative sociology is not the dominant research paradigm in India, one must take notice of the growing interest to study one's own society. In Srinivas's (2004: 418) words, it '... is not unlikely that shortly, information about cultural and social phenomena and their analysis and interpretations, at least in a few Third World countries, is likely to come mostly from the indigenes'. For stressing the indigene-based research, Srinivas (1997: 22), for instance, cited a study in South China: 'Fei was able to produce within two months a first-rate study of a village in South China, an enterprise that would have taken an outsider several years'.

Amidst these reported advantages, there is also a caution provided in the literature. The fieldwork in one's own society '... is far more difficult than fieldwork in an alien society ...' (Srinivas 2004: 413). However, at the same time, the study of one's own society is not only feasible but *essential*, for it is best that culture be studied both by outsiders and insiders. Alone, neither is complete (Srinivas 1997: 22). It must be mentioned that the re-study is a newer research paradigm in India. It can seen in light of the disappearing trend of village studies and ethnographic methods at a time of positivist research trends in the country. The current work on revisiting a classical field site of Sripuram is thus an exploratory research attempt as there is no empirical information available on this village after Béteille's fieldwork (in 1959–60).

Entry into the Site

It is pertinent to mention the reasons for the selection of Sripuram. It was based on month-long visits to various villages in Tamil Nadu in the year 2008. Since the social structure of the village had to have the 'representativeness' of various caste groups, considerable time and energy were invested in finding the best possible field site.[11] In this process, various criteria based on conceptual explorations guided the author.[12] The settlement pattern of the village, especially the social structure, and the social distance between the inhabitants were taken into account in the initial phase. Along with this, the necessary details like the socio-economic statuses, educational and occupational details, and infrastructure and other amenities were gradually gathered.

Consequently, the author has also made use of the different phases of fieldwork both for the collection of primary and secondary data. State-specific education reports, books and other writings on Tamil Nadu were collected. The continuous fieldwork over the years has allowed the author to establish a rapport with the village community as well as with some of the officials in the state. This, to no small extent, facilitated the author to move between both formal and informal ways of interactions with them. Field trips also allowed the author to consult libraries and meet experts on the subject.

Thus, primary data collection took place through participant observation and semi-structured interviews.[13] Based on everyday field notes, reflexive accounts have been documented. Besides, to maintain consistency across sources and informants, the research notes were updated immediately after each day of fieldwork. These offered insights for further analyses. The semi-structured interviews were audio-recorded with the permission of the respondents. These audio files have been transcribed by the author as well as by an external agency for further analyses. These altogether provide empirical support to the field notes and make use of the reflexive process of interpretation.

In light of this, it is pertinent to mention the presence of the author in the field. The author as an 'outsider' at times could not resist giving his perspective when educated un/underemployed youths fail to get a career direction. For instance, the author's interaction with Iyappan, the 33-year-old Pallar EUEY, 'conceptually' helped the latter understand his 'faults' of merely accumulating degrees without 'freedom'. He told the author that he is currently investing his 'waiting period' (for the salaried employment in government service) by concentrating on the contents of the subject instead of escalating his qualification further. Also, Selvam, the 22-year-old non-Brahmin OBC male EUEY, was motivated by the research work on the EUEYs. Recently, he has moved out of the village where he was forced to work in the informal economy. His daily-wage work as a coolie was degrading, as he was forced to take up any job despite the fact that he had a Bachelor's degree in Business Administration. He intended to support his family monetarily. His regular interaction with the author has, however, changed his coping strategies over the years. He also recently reported a 'confident' picture as he went to Chennai in search of a 'matching' job. Thus, ethnography as a critical framework '... remains crucial for an intensive understanding of the local situation, and from this, one spreads out to look at the relations the local communities have with the outside world' (Srivastava 2004: 42–43). This is significant 'in light of the fact that the mainstream quantitative academics (including sociologists) continue to belittle qualitative studies' (Anderson 1999: 452) in the country.

NOTES

1. As quoted in Srivastava (2004: 42).

2. For related ethnographic works, see, for instance, Adler and Adler (1987, 1995); Anderson (1989); Atkinson, Coffey and Delamont (1999); Beals (1978); Brewer (1994); Fine (1993); Foley, Levinson and Hurtig (2001); Hammersley (1985, 1990); Hine (2007); Jenkins (2006); King (2000); Lofland (1995); Lyon (1999); Miller (1994); Ogbu (1981); Preissle and Grant (1998); Sanders (1999); Sarangapani (2003); Stanley (1990); Stoddart (1986); Trujillo (1999); Walford (2001); Whitaker (1996); and Willis and Trondman (2000), among others.

3. Srivastava (2004: 27) lucidly defines observation as '... a *systematic viewing*, which is intentional and planned' (emphasis added).

4. Libraries at Jawaharlal Nehru University, New Delhi; National Institute of Educational Planning and Administration, New Delhi; National Council for Educational Research and Training, New Delhi; University of Madras, Chennai; district libraries in Thanjavur, Pudukkottai and Trichy.

5. According to sociological literature, relative deprivation is a social situation where 'individuals consider themselves deprived when they compare their personal circumstances with those they believe to prevail in their *reference group*' (emphasis added) (Mann 1983: 326).

6. The opinion leaders primarily include influential locals like the panchayat president, village education committee (VEC) members, orphanage administrators and other important people across all castes in the village. Discussion with them had provided the details of the social structure of the village. In addition, the discussion with all the 16 teachers in the local school though has been recorded.

7. Malinowski suggests the importance of maintaining a safe distance from both the influences of the field as well as literature (Adler and Adler 1987; Atkinson and Delamont 2011: 12). The intention is to make use of both primary as well as secondary data to deeply reflect upon to develop a *thick description*.

8. The active phases of the fieldwork were February–March 2009 and August–October 2009. In addition, there were intermittent visits and telephonic follow-ups with the villagers. These were followed by fieldwork in March–May 2010, and again in July–August 2011. The last phase was conducted in March–June 2012.

9. For similar ethnographic research work on India, see, for instance, Ciotti (2006); Dyer (1996a, 1996b, 1997, 2000); Dyer and Choski (1998); Dyer et al. (2004); Fuller and Narashimhan (2007, 2008a, 2008b); Jeffrey (2002, 2009, 2010a, 2010b, 2011); Jeffrey and Dyson (2008); Jeffrey, Jeffrey and Jeffrey (2005, 2010); Sarangapani (2003) and Thapan (2009), among others.

10. As quoted in Madan (1998: 203).

11. An accidental meeting with Professor Béteille in 2018 at the Delhi School of Economics was a turning point.

12. Continuous discussions with Professor Béteille have been most valuable, along with the precious literature on the subject. This has been supported by academic colleagues both in Germany and India.

13. Srivatsava (2004: 452) defines participant observation as a 'technique of observation in which the investigator participates in the social life and organizational activities of the people he/she studies'.

Annexures

Annexure I-A EUYs in Sripuram: Age, Gender, Caste, Class and Qualification

S. No.	*Name*	*Age*	*Gender*	*Caste*	*Class*	*Qualification*
1	Tharani	24	Female	Brahmin	Middle	MA
2	Natesan	36	Male	Brahmin	Lower-middle	B.Com
3	Ambi	59	Male	Brahmin	Lower-middle	SSLC
4	Vasu	39	Male	Brahmin	Upper-middle	HSC
5	Palani	24	Male	OBC	Upper-lower	M.Sc (IT)
6	Kamala	21	Female	SC	Poor	Teacher Training
7	Rambha	26	Female	SC	Poor	MA and M.Phil (Economics)
8	Meena	33	Female	SC	Poor	M.Com
9	Ravikumar	23	Male	SC	Poor	BA and MSW (discontinued)
10	Sri Devi	23	Female	SC	Poor	Nursing course

Source: Author's fieldwork.

Annexure I-B EUYs in Sripuram: Caste and Gender

Caste	*Gender*		*Total*
	Male	*Female*	
Brahmins	3	1	4
OBCs	1	0	1
SC	1	4	5
Total	5	5	10

Source: Author's fieldwork.

Annexure II-A EUEYs in Sripuram: Age, Gender, Caste, Class and Qualification

S. No.	*Name*	*Age*	*Gender*	*Caste*	*Class*	*Qualification*	*Work*
1	Jayanthi	24	Female	Brahmin	Middle	BBA, DCA and typewriting	Para-teacher
2	Raman	39	Male	Brahmin	Lower-middle	B.Com, DCA and typewriting	Purohit
3	Sundaram	23	Male	Forward	Middle	B.Sc	Contract teacher
4	Sunitha	36	Female	OBC	Lower-middle	MA, B.Ed and D.Coop	Headmaster in an unrecognised school
5	Selvam	22	Male	OBC	Poor	BBA	Casual daily-wage labourer
6	Karthi	25	Male	OBC	Middle	BBA and DME	Transition from EUE to EU
7	Kumaran	23	Male	OBC	Middle	Diploma in air-conditioning repair	Agriculturist and AC mechanic

(contd)

Annexure II-A (contd)

S. No.	*Name*	*Age*	*Gender*	*Caste*	*Class*	*Qualification*	*Work*
8	Jeeva	31	Male	OBC	Middle	M.Com (discontinued)	Working in his father's tea stall
9	Iyappan	33	Male	SC	Middle	B.Com, B.PEd, DCA, D.Coop, jewel appraisal, and PG Diploma in Yoga	Para-teacher
10	Mala	24	Female	SC	Poor	BA	NGO
11	Nirmala	28	Female	SC	Poor	BA	NGO
12	Mahesh	25	Male	SC	Poor	BBA	Casual daily-wage labourer
13	Muthu	24	Male	OBC	Poor	BBA	Casual daily-wage labourer

Source: Author's fieldwork.

ANNEXURE II-B EUEYs in Sripuram: Caste and Gender

Caste	*Gender*		*Total*
	Male	*Female*	
Brahmins	2	1	3
OBCs	5	1	6
SC	2	2	4
Total	9	4	13

Note: The data for the Brahmin category also includes one non-Brahmin forward-caste male.

Source: Author's fieldwork.

ANNEXURE III Interview Details

S. No.	*Name*	*Duration*
1	Jayanthi (EUEY)	32:30 minutes
2	Raman (EUEY)	123:99 minutes
3	Sundaram (EUEY)	59:03 minutes
4	Sunitha (EUEY)	09:38 minutes
5	Selvam (EUEY)	35:49 minutes
6	Karthi (EUEY)	26:37 minutes
7	Kumaran (EUEY)	16:51 minutes
8	Jeeva (EUEY)	33:30 minutes
9	Iyappan (EUEY)	67:68 minutes
10	Mala (EUEY)	19:04 minutes
11	Nirmala (EUEY)	24:37 minutes
12	Mahesh (EUEY)	53:56 minutes
13	Muthu	31:37 minutes
14	Kumar (EUEY)	29:57 minutes
15	Tharani (EUY)	24:17 minutes
16	Natesan (EUY)	105:86 minutes
17	Ambi (EUY)	43:27 minutes
18	Vasu (EUY)	34:57 minutes
19	Palani (EUY)	58.50 minutes
20	Kamala (EUY)	09:40 minutes
21	Rambha (EUY)	26:45 minutes
22	Meena (EUY)	16:35 minutes
23	Ravikumar (EUY)	69:19 minutes
24	Sri Devi (EUY)	08:22 minutes
	16 teachers	Roughly 60 minutes each

Source: Author's fieldwork.

Bibliography

'India is the Nation of the Most Unemployed in the World: Labour Bureau Statistics'. 2018. *Outlook*, 5 April. Available at https://www.outlookindia.com/website/story/india-is-the-nation-of-the-most-unemployed-in-the-world-labour-bureau-statistics/310545 (accessed 10 May 2020).

'School Lunch: Unpalatable Carrots', editorial. 2001. *Economic and Political Weekly* 36 (25): 2208–09.

'School Meals: Food for Thought', editorial. 2002. *Economic and Political Weekly* 37 (37): 3772–73.

'TRIBES: Ethics of Research', editorial. 2003. *Economic and Political Weekly* 38 (41): 4284.

Adler, Patricia A., and Peter Adler. 1987. 'The Past and the Future of Ethnography'. *Journal of Contemporary Ethnography* 16 (1): 4–24.

———. 1995. 'The Demography of Ethnography'. *Journal of Contemporary Ethnography* 24 (1): 3–29.

Afridi, Farzana. 2005. 'Midday Meals in Two States: Comparing the Financial and Institutional Organisation of the Programme'. *Economic and Political Weekly* 40 (15): 1528–34.

Ahmad, Shakeel. 2000. 'Traditions of Learning and Modernisation: A Case of Machhti, Ghazipur, U.P.'. Operation Blackboard Project: An Ethnographic Study, National Institute of Educational Planning and Administration, New Delhi.

Alkire, Sabina. 2002. *Valuing Freedoms: Sen's Capability Approach and Poverty Reduction*. Oxford: Oxford University Press.

Allan, George. 2003. 'A Critique of Using Grounded Theory as a Research Method'. Department of Information Systems and Computer Applications, Portsmouth University, UK.

Ambedkar, B. R. 2014. *Annihilation of Caste*. UK: Verso.

Anderson, Gary L. 1989. 'Critical Ethnography in Education: Origins, Current Status, and New Directions'. *Review of Educational Research* 59 (3): 249–70.

Anderson, Leon. 1999. 'The Open Road to Ethnography's Future'. *Journal of Contemporary Ethnography* 28 (5): 451–59.

Apthorpe, Raymond. 1997. 'Human Development Reporting and Social Anthropology'. *Social Anthropology* 5 (1): 21–34.

Aschaffenburg, Karen and Ineke Maas. 1997. 'Cultural and Educational Careers: The Dynamics of Social Reproduction'. *American Sociological Review* 62 (4): 573–87.

Atkinson, Paul and Martyn Hammersley. 1994. *Handbook of Qualitative Research*. London: Sage Publications.

Atkinson, Paul and Sara Delamont (eds). 2011. *Sage Qualitative Research Methods*. New Delhi: Sage.

Atkinson, Paul, Amanda Coffey and Sara Delamont. 1999. 'Ethnography: Post, Past, and the Present'. *Journal of Contemporary Ethnography* 28 (5): 460–71.

Aturupane, Harsha, Paul Glewwe and Paul Isenman. 1994. 'Poverty, Human Development, and Growth: An Emerging Consensus?'. *American Economic Review* 84 (2): 244–49.

Aylward, Carol A. 2010. 'Intersectionality: Crossing the Theoretical and Praxis Divide'. *Journal of Critical Race Inquiry* 1 (1): 1–48.

Ayres, Ron and Manuela Torrijos Simon. 2003. 'Education, Poverty and Sustainable Livelihoods in Tamil Nadu: Inequalities, Opportunities and Constraints'. *Review of Political Economy* 15 (2): 211–29.

Ayyar, Vaidyanatha R. V. 2005. 'What Lessons Can DPEP Offer?'. *Journal of Educational Planning and Administration* 19 (1): 49–65.

Bajpai, Nirupam and Sangeeta Goyal. 2004. 'Primary Education in India: Quality and Coverage Issues'. CGSD Working Paper No. 11, The Earth Institute, Columbia University.

Balasubramanian, K., P. Tamizoli and S. Murugakani. 2002. 'Labour, Market Linkages and Gender: Case Study of a Village in Tamil Nadu'. *Economic and Political Weekly* 37 (43), 26 October: 4390–96.

Banerji, Rukmini. 1997. 'Why Don't Children Complete Primary School: A Case Study of a Low-income Neighbourhood in Delhi'. *Economic and Political Weekly* 32 (32): 2053–63.

_____. 2000. 'Poverty and Primary Schooling: Field Studies from Mumbai and Delhi'. *Economic and Political Weekly* 35 (10): 795–802.

Bawane, Jyoti. 2000. 'A Rural School Experience: Space for Dynamic Movement, a Case of Masod Village in Maharashtra'. Operation Blackboard Project: An Ethnographic Study, National Institute of Educational Planning and Administration, New Delhi.

Beals, Alan R. 1964. Review of '*When Caste Barriers Fall: A Study of Social and Economic Change in a South Indian Village* by Dagfinn Sivertsen'. *American Anthropologist* 66 (6), part 1: 1429.

Beals, Alan R. 1970. 'Namahalli, 1953–1966: Urban Influence and Change in Southern Mysore'. In *Change and Continuity in India's Villages*, ed. K. Ishwaran, 57–72. New York: Columbia University Press.

———. 1978. 'The Remembered Village as Ethnography'. *Contributions to Indian Sociology* 12 (1): 109–15.

Bebbington, Anthony. 1999. 'Capitals and Capabilities: A Framework for Analyzing Peasant Viability, Rural Livelihoods and Poverty'. *World Development* 27 (12): 2021–44.

Becker, Gary S. 1962. 'Investment in Human Capital: A Theoretical Analysis'. *The Journal of Political Economy* 70 (5): 9–49.

———. 1964. *Human Capital: A Theoretical and Empirical Analysis, with Special Reference to Education*. US: Columbia University Press.

Becker, Gary S., and Nigel Tomes. 1986. 'Human Capital and the Rise and Fall of Families'. *Journal of Labor Economics* 4 (3): S1–39.

Beegle, Kathleen, Joachim Weerdt and Stefan Dercon. 2010. 'Orphanhood and Human Capital Destruction: Is There Persistence into Adulthood?'. *Demography* 47 (1), February: 163–80.

Bell, Daniel. 1977. 'On Meritocracy and Equality'. In *Power and Ideology in Education*, ed. Jerome Karabel and A. H. Halsey, 609–35. New York: Oxford University Press.

Berger, Michele Tracy and Kathleen Guidroz (eds). 2009. *The Intersectional Approach: Transforming the Academy through Race, Class, and Gender*. US: University of North Carolina Press.

Berger, Peter L., and Thomas Luckmann. 1966. *The Social Construction of Reality: A Treatise in the Sociology of Knowledge*. England: Penguin Books.

Berreman, G. D. 2011. 'Ethnography: Method and Product'. In *Methodology and Fieldwork: Oxford in Indian Readings in Sociology and Social Anthropology*, ed. Vinay K. Srivastava, 157–90. New Delhi: Oxford University Press.

Berry, Sara. 1985. *Fathers Work for Their Sons: Accumulation, Mobility, and Class Formation in an Extended Yorùbá Community*. California: University of California Press.

Béteille, André. 1964. 'A Note on the Pongal Festival in a Tanjore Village'. *Man* 64: 73–75.

———. 1965a. *Caste, Class, and Power: Changing Patterns of Stratification in a Tanjore Village*. Berkeley and Los Angeles: University of California Press.

———. 1965b. 'Social Organisation of Temples in a Tanjore Village'. *History of Religions* 5 (1): 74–92.

———. 1972a. 'Agrarian Relations in Tanjore District, South India'. *Sociological Bulletin* 21 (2): 122–51.

———. 1972b. 'Pollution and Poverty'. In *The Untouchable in Contemporary India*, ed. J. Michael Mahar, 411–20. US: The University of Arizona Press.

Béteille, André. 1972c. 'The Tribulations of Fieldwork'. *Economic and Political Weekly* 7 (31–33): 1509–16.

_____. 1974. *Studies in Agrarian Social Structure*. New Delhi: Oxford University Press.

_____. 1983. *Equality and Inequality: Theory and Practice*. New Delhi: Oxford University Press.

_____. 1986. 'Food, Economics and Entitlements'. Working paper no. 1, World Institute for Development Economics Research, United Nations University.

_____. 1990. 'Some Observations on the Comparative Method'. *Economic and Political Weekly* 25 (40): 2255–63.

_____. 1993. 'Amartya Sen's Utopia'. *Economic and Political Weekly* 28 (16): 753–56.

_____. 2001. 'Equality and Individual Achievement'. *Economic and Political Weekly* 36 (45): 4271–75.

_____. 2002. *Sociology: Essays on Approach and Method*. New Delhi: Oxford University Press.

_____. 2003. 'Poverty and Inequality'. *Economic and Political Weekly* 38 (42): 4455–63.

_____. 2007. 'The School and the Community'. *Journal of Educational Planning and Administration* 21 (3): 191–201.

_____. 2009a. *Caste, Class and Power: Changing Patterns of Stratification in a Tanjore Village* (second edition/sixth impression). New Delhi: Oxford University Press.

_____. 2009b. *Marxism and Class Analysis* (second edition/sixth impression). New Delhi: Oxford University Press.

_____. 2011. 'Foreword'. In *Who Goes to School?: Exploring Exclusion in Indian Education*, ed. R. Govinda, *xvii–xix*. New Delhi: Oxford University Press.

_____. 2012. *Caste, Class and Power: Changing Patterns of Stratification in a Tanjore Village*. New Delhi: Oxford India Perennials, Oxford University Press.

Betraux, Daniel and Paul Thompson. 1997. *Pathways to Social Class: A Qualitative Approach to Social Mobility*. Oxford: Clarendon Press.

Bhatty, Kiran. 1998a. 'Educational Deprivation in India: A Survey of Field Investigations'. *Economic and Political Weekly* 33 (27): 1731–40.

_____. 1998b. 'Educational Deprivation in India: A Survey of Field Investigations'. *Economic and Political Weekly* 33 (28): 1858–68.

Bhaumik, Sumon K., and Manisha Chakrabarty. 2011. 'Whither Human Capital?: The Woeful Tale of Transition to Tertiary Education in India'. Working paper no. 1019, William Davidson Institute, University of Michigan.

Borgatta, Edgar F., and Rhonda J. V. Montgomery. 2000. *Encyclopedia of Sociology*, (second edition). New York: Macmillan Reference.

Bowleg, Lisa. 2008. 'When Black + Lesbian + Woman ≠ Black Lesbian Woman: The Methodological Challenges of Qualitative and Quantitative Intersectionality Research'. *Sex Roles* 59 (5): 312–25.

Bowles, Samuel and Herbert Gintis. 1976. *Schooling in Capitalist America: Educational Reform and the Contradictions of Economic Life*. New York: Basic Books.

———. 1988a. 'Contradiction and Reproduction in Educational Theory'. In *Bowles and Gintis Revisited: Correspondence and Contradiction in Educational Theory*, ed. Mike Cole, 16–32. UK: The Falmer Press.

———. 1988b. 'Prologue: The Correspondence Principle'. In *Bowles and Gintis Revisited: Correspondence and Contradiction in Educational Theory*, ed. Mike Cole, 1–4. UK: The Falmer Press.

Bowles, Samuel, Herbert Gintis and Melissa Osborne Groves (eds). 2005a. 'Introduction'. In *Unequal Chances: Family Background and Economic Success*, 1–22. Princeton: Princeton University Press.

——— (eds). 2005b. *Unequal Chances: Family Background and Economic Success*. Princeton: Princeton University Press.

Bredström, Anna. 2006. 'Intersectionality: A Challenge for Feminist HIV/AIDS Research?'. *European Journal of Women's Studies* 13 (3): 229–43.

Breman, Jan. 1974. *Patronage and Exploitation: Changing Agrarian Relations in South Gujarat, India*. California: University of California Press.

———. 1987. *The Informal Sector in Research: Theory and Practice*. Rotterdam: The Comparative Asian Studies Programme (CASP), Erasmus University.

———. 1988. *The Shattered Image: Construction and Deconstruction of the Village in Colonial Asia*. The Netherlands: Foris Publications Holland.

———. 1996. *Footloose Labour: Working in India's Informal Economy*. Great Britain: Cambridge University Press.

———. 2004. 'Return of Social Inequality: A Fashionable Doctrine'. *Economic and Political Weekly* 39 (35): 3869–72.

———. 2010. 'India's Social Question in a State of Denial'. *Economic and Political Weekly* 45 (23): 42–46.

Brewer, John D. 1994. 'The Ethnographic Critique of Ethnography: Sectarianism in the RUC'. *Sociology* 28 (1): 231–44.

Bridges, David. 2006. 'Adaptive Preference, Justice and Identity in the Context of Widening Participation in Higher Education'. *Ethics and Education* 1 (1): 15–28.

Bruckner, Donald W. 2009. 'In Defense of Adaptive Preferences'. *Philosophical Studies* 142 (3): 307–24.

Bull, Rodney and Ian Shaw. 1992. 'Constructing Causal Accounts in Social Work'. *Sociology* 26 (4): 635–49.

Caillods, Francoise. 1998. 'Education Strategies for Disadvantaged Groups: Some Basic Issues'. IIEP contributions no. 31, International Institute for Educational Planning, Paris.

Caldwell, John C., P. H. Reddy and Pat Caldwell. 1985. 'Educational Transition in Rural South India'. *Population and Development Review* 11 (1): 29–51.

Cassidy, Wanda and Margaret Jackson. 2005. 'The Need for Equality in Education: An Intersectionality Examination of Labeling and Zero Tolerance Practices'. *McGill Journal of Education* 40 (3): 435–56.

Chambers, Robert. 1981. 'Rural Poverty Unperceived: Problems and Remedies'. *World Development* 9 (1): 1–19.

Chanana, Karuna. 1993. 'Accessing Higher Education: The Dilemma of Schooling Women, Minorities, Scheduled Castes and Scheduled Tribes in Contemporary India'. *Higher Education* 26 (1): 69–92.

Chauhan, I. S. 1967. Review of '*Caste, Class, and Power: Changing Patterns of Stratification in a Tanjore Village* by André Béteille'. *Economic and Political Weekly* 2 (25): 1119–20.

Choo, Hae Yeon and Myra Marx Ferree. 2010. 'Practicing Intersectionality in Sociological Research: A Critical Analysis of Inclusions, Interactions, and Institutions in the Study of Inequalities'. *Sociological Theory* 28 (2): 129–49.

Chopra, Radhika and Patricia Jeffery (eds). 2005. *Educational Regimes in Contemporary India*. New Delhi: Sage Publications.

Ciotti, Manuela. 2006. '"In the Past We Were a Bit 'Chamar'": Education as a Self- and Community Engineering Process in Northern India'. *Journal of the Royal Anthropological Institute* 12 (4): 899–916.

Clark-Deces, Isabelle (ed.). 2011a. *A Companion to the Anthropology of India*. UK: Wiley-Blackwell.

_____. 2011b. 'The Decline of Dravidian Kinship in Local Perspectives'. In *A Companion to the Anthropology of India*, ed. Isabelle Clark-Deces, 517–35. UK: Wiley-Blackwell.

Cleaver, Frances. 2005. 'The Inequality of Social Capital and the Reproduction of Chronic Poverty'. *World Development* 33 (6): 893–906.

Cole, Elizabeth R. 2008. 'Coalitions as a Model for Intersectionality: From Practice to Theory'. *Sex Roles* 59 (5–6): 443–53.

_____. 2009. 'Intersectionality and Research in Psychology'. *American Psychologist* 64 (3): 170–80.

Cole, Mike (ed.). 1988. *Bowles and Gintis Revisited: Correspondence and Contradiction in Educational Theory*. UK: The Falmer Press.

Coleman, J., United States Office of Education and National Center for Education Statistics. 1966. *Equality of Educational Opportunity*. Washington: Department of Health, Education and Welfare.

Coleman, James S. 1988. 'Social Capital in the Creation of Human Capital'. *American Journal of Sociology* 94, supplement: S95–120.

Collins, Stephanie Baker. 2005. 'An Understanding of Poverty from Those Who Are Poor'. *Action Research* 3 (1): 9–31.

Connell, R. W. 1994. 'Poverty and Education'. *Harvard Educational Review* 64 (2), summer: 125–49.

Conwill, William Louis. 2010. 'Domestic Violence Among the Black Poor: Intersectionality and Social Justice'. *International Journal for the Advancement of Counselling* 32 (1): 31–45.

Corbridge, Stuart, Glyn Williams, Manoj Kumar Srivastava and Véron René. 2005. *Seeing the State: Governance and Governmentality in India*. UK: Cambridge University Press.

Cudd, Ann E. 2011. Review of '*Adaptive Preferences and Women's Empowerment* by Serene J. Khader'. *Notre Dame Philosophical Reviews*, November.

D'Souza, Victors. 1979. 'Socio-cultural Marginality: A Theory of Urban Slums and Poverty in India'. *Sociological Bulletin* 28 (1–2): 9–24.

———. 1999. Review of '*Caste, Class, and Power: Changing Patterns of Stratification in a Tanjore Village* by André Béteille'. *Sociological Bulletin* 48 (1–2): 298–302.

Das, Amarendra. 2007. 'How Far Have We come in Sarva Shiksha Abhiyan?'. *Economic and Political Weekly* 42 (1), January: 21–23.

Das, Veena (ed.). 2004. *Oxford Handbook of Indian Sociology*. New Delhi: Oxford University Press.

Davenport, William. 1964. Review of '*When Caste Barriers Fall: A Study of Social and Economic Change in a South Indian Village* by Dagfinn Sivertsen'. *Science* 145 (3629): 257.

Davies, Philip. 2000. 'The Relevance of Systematic Reviews to Educational Policy and Practice'. *Oxford Review of Education* 26 (3–4): 365–78.

Davis, Kathy. 2008. 'Intersectionality as Buzzword: A Sociology of Science Perspective on What Makes a Feminist Theory Successful'. *Feminist Theory* 9 (1): 67–85.

De, Anuradha, Tanuka Endow and Sourindra Ghosh. 2010. 'Educational Outcomes and Poverty: Some Findings from a Household Survey in Rajasthan and Madhya Pradesh'. Working paper no. 32, Research Consortium of Educational Outcomes and Poverty (RECOUP).

Dean, Hartley. 2009. 'Critiquing Capabilities: The Distractions of a Beguiling Concept'. *Critical Social Policy* 29 (2): 261–78.

Deaton, Angus and Jean Drèze. 2002. 'Poverty and Inequality in India: A Re-examination'. *Economic and Political Weekly* 37 (36): 3729–48.

Deem, Rosemary. 1996. 'The Future of Educational Research in the Context of the Social Sciences: A Special Case?'. *British Journal of Educational Studies* 44 (2): 143–58.

Deliege, Robert. 2011. 'Caste, Class and Untouchability'. In A *Companion to the Anthropology of India*, ed. Isabelle Clark-Deces, 45–61. UK: Wiley-Blackwell.

Deneulin, Severine and J. Allister McGregor. 2010. 'The Capabilities Approach and the Politics of a Social Conception of Wellbeing'. *European Journal of Social Theory* 13 (4): 501–19.

Denzin, Norman K., and Yvonna S. Lincoln (eds). 2005. *The Sage Handbook of Qualitative Research*. US: Sage Publications.

Department of Elementary Education and Literacy, n.d. 'Sarva Shiksha Abhiyan: Framework for Implementation'. Ministry of Human Resource Development, New Delhi.

Desai, Meghnad. 1991. 'Human Development: Concepts and Measurement'. *European Economic Review* 35 (2–3): 350–57.

Deshpande, Ashwini. 2008. 'Caste and Diversity in India'. In *The Elgar Companion to Social Economics*, ed. John B. Davis and Wilfred Dlfsma, 198–212. UK: Edward Elgar.

Deuchar, Andrew. 2014. 'All Dressed Up with Nowhere to Go: Transitions to (Un)Employment for Lower Middle Class Young Men'. *Economic and Political Weekly* 49 (17): 104–11.

Devakumar, J. 2017. 'Caste Clashes and Dalits Rights Violations in Tamil Nadu'. *Social Scientist* 35 (11–12): 39–54.

DiMaggio, Paul. 1982. 'Cultural Capital and School Success: The Impact of Status Culture Participation on the Grades of U.S. High School Students'. *American Sociological Review* 47 (2): 189–201.

DiMaggio, Paul and John Mohr. 1985. 'Cultural Capital, Educational Attainment, and Marital Selection'. *The American Journal of Sociology* 90 (6): 1231–61.

Dore, Ronald. 1976. *The Diploma Disease: Education, Qualification and Development*. London: George Allen and Unwin.

Drèze, Jean. 2002. 'On Research and Action'. *Economic and Political Weekly* 37 (9): 817–19.

_____. 2004a. 'Democracy and Right to Food'. *Economic and Political Weekly* 39 (17): 1723–31.

_____. 2004b. 'Patterns of Literacy and their Social Context'. In *Oxford Handbook of Indian Sociology*, ed. Veena Das, 345–61. New Delhi: Oxford University Press.

Drèze, Jean and Amartya Sen. 1997. *Indian Development: Selected Regional Perspectives*. Delhi: Oxford University Press.

_____. 1999. *The Amartya Sen and Jean Drèze Omnibus* (comprises three volumes: *Poverty and Famines*; *Hunger and Public Action*; and *India: Economic Development and Social Opportunity*). New Delhi: Oxford University Press.

Drèze, Jean and Aparajita Goyal. 2003. 'The Future of Mid-day Meals'. *Economic and Political Weekly* 38 (44): 4673–83.

Drèze, Jean and Geeta Gandhi Kingdon. 1999. 'School Participation in Rural India'. The Development Economics Discussion Paper Series no. 18, London School of Economics, UK.

Driver, Edwin D. 1982. 'Class, Caste, and "Status Summation" in Urban South India'. *Contributions to Indian Sociology* 16 (2): 225–53.

Dumais, Susan A. 2002. 'Cultural Capital, Gender, and School Success: The Role of Habitus'. *Sociology of Education* 75 (1): 44–68.

Duncan, Greg, Ariel Kalil, Susan E. Mayer, Robin Tepper and Monique R. Payne. 2005. 'The Apple Does not Fall Far from the Tree'. In *Unequal Chances: Family Background and Economic Success*, ed. Samuel Bowles, Herbert Gintis and Melissa Osborne Groves, 23–79. Princeton: Princeton University Press.

Duneier, Mitchell. 1992. *Slim's Table: Race, Respectability, and Masculinity*. Chicago: The University of Chicago Press.

Dunn, D. 1993. 'Gender Inequality in Education and Employment in the Scheduled Castes and Tribes of India'. *Population Research and Policy Review* 12 (1): 53–70.

Dunne, Máiréad and Louise Gazeley. 2008. 'Teachers, Social Class and Underachievement'. *British Journal of Sociology of Education* 29 (5): 451–63.

Dyer, Caroline. 1996a. 'Primary Teachers and Policy Innovation in India: Some Neglected Issues'. *International Journal of Educational Development* 16 (1): 27–40.

——. 1996b. 'The Improvement of Primary School Quality in India: Successes and Failures of Operation Blackboard'. Edinburgh Papers in South Asian Studies no. 4, University of Edinburgh.

——. 1997. 'Operation Blackboard: Policy Implementation in Indian Elementary Education'. PhD thesis, University of Edinburgh, UK.

——. 2000. 'Education for All and the Rabaris of Kachchh, Western India'. *International Journal of Educational Research* 33 (3): 241–51.

Dyer, Caroline and Archana Choski. 1998. 'Education is Like Wearing Glasses: Nomads' Views of Literacy and Empowerment'. *International Journal of Educational Development* 18 (5): 405–13.

Dyer, Caroline, Archana Choksi, Vinita Awasty, Uma Iyer, Renu Moyade, Neerja Nigam, Neetu Purohit, Swati Shah and Swati Sheth. 2004. 'Knowledge for Teacher Development in India: The Importance of "Local Knowledge" for In-service Education'. *International Journal of Educational Development* 24 (1): 39–52.

Dyer, Caroline, Archana Choski, Vinita Awasty and Uma Iyer. 2004. *District Institutes of Education and Training: A Comparative Study in Three Indian*

States. UK: Department for International Development: Educational Papers.

Elster, Jon. 2016. *Sour Grapes Studies in the Subversion of Rationality*. UK: Cambridge University Press.

Epstein, Scarlett. 1967. Review of '*Caste, Class, and Power: Changing Patterns of Stratification in a Tanjore Village* by André Béteille'. *American Ethnologist*, New Series 69 (2): 245–46.

Etienne, Gilbert. 1968. *Studies in Indian Agriculture: The Art of the Possible*, trans. Megan Mothersole. California: University of California Press.

Faist, Thomas. 1993. 'From School to Work: Public Policy and Underclass Formation among Young Turks in Germany during the 1980s'. *International Migration Review* 27 (2): 306–31.

Fine, Gary Alan. 1993. 'Ten Lies of Ethnography: Moral Dilemmas of Field Research'. *Journal of Contemporary Ethnography* 22 (3): 267–94.

Foley, Douglas A., Bradley A. Levinson and Janise Hurtig. 2000. 'Anthropology Goes Inside: The New Educational Ethnography of Ethnicity and Gender'. *Review of Research in Education* 25 (1): 37–98.

Fonseca, A. J. (ed.). 1971. *Challenge of Poverty in India*. Delhi: Vikas Publications.

Fukuda-Parr, Sakiko. 2003. 'The Human Development Paradigm: Operationalising Sen's Ideas on Capabilities'. *Feminist Economics* 9 (2–3): 301–17.

_____. 2011. 'Theory and Policy in International Development: Human Development and Capabilities Approach and the Millennium Development Goals'. *International Studies Review* 13 (1): 122–32.

Fukuda-Parr, Sakiko and A. K. Shiva Kumar (eds). 2003. *Readings in Human Development: Concepts, Measures and Policies for a Development Paradigm*. New Delhi: Oxford University Press.

Fuller, C. J. 1983. Review of '*Rural Society in Southeast India* by Kathleen Gough'. *Man* 18 (3): 614–15.

_____. 2011. 'The Modern Transformation of an Old Elite: The Case of the Tamil Brahmins'. In *A Companion to the Anthropology of India*, ed. Isabelle Clark-Deces, 80–97. UK: Wiley-Blackwell.

_____. 2012. 'Introduction'. In André Béteille, *Caste, Class and Power* (second edition/sixth impression). New Delhi: Oxford India Perennials, Oxford University Press.

Fuller, C. J., and Haripriya Narasimhan. 2007. 'Information Technology Professionals and the New-rich Middle Class in Chennai (Madras)'. *Modern Asian Studies* 41 (1): 121–50.

_____. 2008a. 'Companionate Marriage in India: The Changing Marriage System in a Middle-class Brahman Subcaste'. *Journal of the Royal Anthropological Institute* 14 (4): 736–54.

Fuller, C. J., and Haripriya Narasimhan. 2008b. 'From Landlords to Software Engineers: Migration and Urbanisation among Tamil Brahmans'. *Comparative Studies in Society and History* 50 (1): 170–96.

Gang, Ira N., Kunal Sen and Myeong-Su Yun. 2004. 'Caste, Ethnicity and Poverty in Rural India'. Tulane University.

Gasper, Des. 2002. 'Is Sen's Capabilities approach an Adequate Basis for Considering Human Development'. *Review of Political Economy* 14 (4): 435–61.

———. 2007. 'What is the Capabilities Approach?: Its Core, Rationale, Partners and Dangers'. *The Journal of Socio-economics* 36 (3): 335–59.

Gautam, Indra. 2000. 'Educational Perspectives in the Eastern Slopes: A Case Study of Sihphir Village, Mizoram'. Operation Blackboard Project: An Ethnographic Study, National Institute of Educational Planning and Administration, New Delhi.

Geertz, Clifford. 1973. *The Interpretation of Cultures*. US: Basic Books.

George, Ann. 2010. 'Towards Holistic Understanding of the Lives of the Poor: Reading the Life History of Viramma (a Poor Dalit Woman) Conjointly with Martha Nussbaum's List of Capabilities'. *Indian Journal of Human Development* 4 (2): 351–67.

Gilbertson, Amanda. 2014. '"Mugging Up" versus "Exposure": International Schools and Social Mobility in Hyderabad, India'. *Ethnography and Education* 9 (2): 210–23.

Gilead, Tal. 2009. 'Human Capital, Education and the Promotion of Social Cooperation: A Radical Critique'. *Studies in Philosophy and Education* 28 (6): 555–67.

Gist, Noel P. 1954. 'Caste Differentials in South India'. *American Sociological Review* 19 (2): 126–37.

Goffman, Erving. 1959. *The Presentation of Self in Everyday Life*. New York: Anchor Books.

———. 1967. *Asylum: Essays on the Social Situation of Mental Patients and Other Inmates*. Penguin: Harmondsworth.

Gorringe, H., R. Jeffrey and S. Sariola. 2009. 'Ethnographic Insights into Enduring Inequalities'. *Journal of South Asian Development* 4 (1): 1–6.

Gough, Kathleen. 1971. *Aspects of Caste in South India, Ceylon and North-west Pakistan*. Great Britain: Cambridge University Press.

———. 1981. *Rural Society in Southeast India*. US: Cambridge University Press.

Government of India. 2002. 'National Human Development Report 2001'. Planning Commission, New Delhi.

———. 2008–09. 'Enrolment-based Indicators'. Unified District Information System for School Education. Available at http://udise.in/Downloads/Publications/Publications%202008-09/AR%202008-09/Enrolment-Based%20Indicators.pdf (accessed 16 September 2014).

Government of India. 2011. *India Human Development Report 2011: Towards Social Inclusion*. New Delhi: Oxford University Press.

____. 2012–13. Ministry of Human Resource Development Annual Report, New Delhi.

Government of Tamil Nadu. 2003. *Tamil Nadu Human Development Report*. Delhi: Social Science Press.

Govinda, R. 2011. *Who Goes to School?: Exploring Exclusion in Indian Education*. New Delhi: Oxford University Press.

Grabham, Emily, Davina Cooper, Jane Krishnadas and Didi Herman (eds). 2009. *Intersectionality and Beyond: Law, Power and the Politics of Location*. US: Routledge-Cavendish.

Gray, Hugh. 1965. Review of '*When Caste Barriers Fall: A Study of Social and Economic Change in a South Indian Village* by Dagfinn Sivertsen'. *The British Journal of Sociology* 16 (3), September: 276–77.

____. 1967. Review of '*Caste, Class, and Power: Changing Patterns of Stratification in a Tanjore Village* by André Béteille'. *Bulletin of the School of Oriental and African Studies* (University of London) 30 (1): 251.

Greene, Robert and Joost Elffers. 1999. *The 48 Laws of Power*. New Delhi: Viva Books Private Limited.

Guhan, S. 1984. Review of '*Rural Society in Southeast India* by Kathleen Gough'. *American Anthropologist* 86 (1), March: 209–10.

Gupta, Dipankar (ed.). 1991. *Social Stratification*. New Delhi: Oxford University Press.

____. 2009. *The Caged Phoenix: Can India Fly?*. New Delhi: Penguin Books India.

Gupta, Shiv Prakash. 1984. 'Conceptualising Poverty'. *Sociological Bulletin* 33 (1–2): 63–74.

Guru, Gopal. 2002. 'How Egalitarian are the Social Science in India?'. *Economic and Political Weekly* 37 (50): 5003–09.

Hammersley, Martyn. 1985. 'From Ethnography to Theory: A Programme and Paradigm in the Sociology of Education'. *Sociology* 19 (2): 244–59.

____. 1990. 'What's Wrong with Ethnography?: The Myth of Theoretical Description'. *Sociology* 24 (4): 597–615.

____. 2003. 'Social Research Today: Some Dilemmas and Distinctions'. *Qualitative Social Work* 2 (1): 25–44.

Hancock, Ange-Marie. 2007. 'When Multiplication Doesn't Equal Quick Addition: Examining Intersectionality as a Research Paradigm'. *Perspectives on Politics* 5 (1): 63–79.

Hankivsky, Olena and Renee Cormier. 2010. 'Intersectionality and Public Policy: Some Lessons from Existing Models'. *Political Research Quarterly* 20 (10): 1–13.

Haq, Mahbub ul. 2003.'The Birth of the Human Development Index'. In *Readings in Human Development*, ed. Sakiko Fukuda-Parr and A. K. Shiva Kumar, 127–37. Oxford: Oxford University Press.

Harriss, John. 1986. 'The Working Poor and the Labour Aristocracy in a South Indian City: A Descriptive and Analytical Account'. *Modern Asian Studies* 20 (2): 231–83.

——. 1998. 'Development Studies and the Development of India: An Awkward Case?'. *Oxford Development Studies* 26 (3): 287–309.

——. 2007. 'Bringing Politics Back into Poverty Analysis: Why Understanding Social Relations Matters More for Policy on Chronic Poverty than Measurement'. Working paper no. 77, Chronic Poverty Research Centre (CPRC), UK.

Harriss-White, Barbara and K. S. Subramanian (eds). 1999. *Illfare in India: Essays on India's Social Sector in Honour of S. Guhan*. New Delhi: Sage Publications.

——. 2003. *India Working: Essays on Society and Economy*. UK: Cambridge University Press.

Hart, C. S. 2012. Review of '*Amartya Sen's Capabilities Approach and Social Justice in Education*'. *British Journal of Sociology of Education* 33 (4): 607–13.

Hicks, Norman L. 1980. 'Is There a Tradeoff between Growth and Basic Needs'. In *Poverty and Basic Needs*, 22–25. Washington, D.C.: World Bank.

Hicks, Norman and Paul Streeten. 1979. 'Indicators of Development: The Search for a Basic Needs Yardstick'. *World Development* 7 (6): 567–80.

Hill, Elizabeth, Meera Samson and Shyamasree Dasgupta. 2011. 'Expanding the School Market in India: Parental Choice and the Reproduction of Social Inequality'. *Economic and Political Weekly* 46 (35): 98–105.

Hinchcliffe, Geoffrey and Lorella Terzi. 2009. 'Introduction to the Special Issue "Capabilities and Education"'. *Studies in Philosophy and Education* 28 (5): 387–90.

Hinchliffe, Geoffrey William and Adrienne Jolly. 2011. 'Graduate Identity and Employability'. *British Educational Research Journal* 37 (4): 563–84.

Hine, Christine, n.d. 'Virtual Ethnography'. Centre for Research into Innovation, Culture and Technology, Brunel University, UK.

——. 2007. 'Multi-sited Ethnography as a Middle Range Methodology for Contemporary STS'. *Science, Technology and Human Values* 32 (6): 652–71.

Ho Sui-Chu, Esther and J. Douglas Willms. 1996. 'Effects of Parental Involvement on Eighth-grade Achievement'. *Sociology of Education* 69 (2): 126–41.

Hockings, Paul. 1977. 'The Abbe Dubois, an early French Ethnographer'. *Contributions to Indian Sociology* 11 (2): 329–43.

Hopkins, Michael. 1991. 'Human Development Revisited', UNDP report. *World Development* 19 (10): 1469–73.

Howe, Kenneth R., and Michele S. Moses. 1999. 'Ethics in Educational Research'. *Review of Research in Education* 24 (1): 21–59.

Ishwaran, K. (ed.). 1970a. *Change and Continuity in India's Villages*. New York: Columbia University Press.

____ (ed.). 1970b. 'Mallur: Internal Dynamics of Change in a Mysore Village'. In *Change and Continuity in India's Villages*, 165–95. New York: Columbia University Press.

Islam, Maidul. 2011. 'Flawed Idea of Justice'. *Economic and Political Weekly* 46 (32): 116–21.

Jackson, William A. 2005. 'Capabilities, Culture and Social Structure'. *Review of Social Economy* 63 (1): 101–24.

____. 2009. *Economics, Culture and Social Theory*. UK: Edward Elgar.

Jami, Froagh Ahmad. 2000. 'School No Man's Land: A Qualitative Account of "School and Society Relationship" in Kheria Village (in Hardoi District of U.P.)'. Operation Blackboard Project: An Ethnographic Study, National Institute of Educational Planning and Administration, New Delhi.

Jayaraj, D., and S. Subramanian. 2005. 'Out of School and (Probably) in Work: Child Labour and Capability Deprivation in India'. Research paper no. 2005/55, UNU-WIDER, United Nations University.

Jayaram, N. 1977. 'Higher Education as a Status Stabilizer: Students in Bangalore'. *Contributions to India Sociology* 11 (1): 169–91.

Jeffrey, Craig. 2002. 'Caste, Class, and Clientelism: A Political Economy of Everyday Corruption in Rural North India'. *Economic Geography* 78 (1): 21–41.

____. 2009. 'Fixing Futures: Educated Unemployment through a North Indian Lens'. *Comparative Studies in Society and History* 51 (1): 182–211.

____. 2010a. *Timepass: Youth, Class, and the Politics of Waiting in India*. California: Stanford University Press.

____. 2010b. 'Timepass: Youth, Class and Time among Unemployed Young Men in India'. *American Ethnologist* 37 (3): 465–81.

____. 2011. 'Great Expectations: Youth in Contemporary India'. In *A Companion to the Anthropology of India*, ed. Isabelle Clark-Deces, 62–79. UK: Wiley-Blackwell.

Jeffrey, Craig and Jane Dyson. 2008. *Telling Young Lives: Portraits of Global Youth*. Philadelphia: Temple University Press.

Jeffrey, Craig, Patricia Jeffery and Roger Jeffery. 2005. 'When Schooling Fails: Young Men, Education and Low-caste Politics in Rural North India'. *Contributions to India Sociology* 39 (1): 1–37.

Jeffrey, Craig, Patricia Jeffery and Roger Jeffery. 2010. *Education, Unemployment and Masculinities in India*. New Delhi: Social Science Press and Orient BlackSwan.

Jenkins, Tim. 2006. 'Bourdieu's Bearnais Ethnography'. *Theory, Culture and Society* 23 (6): 45–72.

Jha, Jyotsna and Dhir Jhingran. 2005. *Elementary Education for the Poorest and Other Deprived Groups: The Real Challenge of Universalization*. New Delhi: Manohar Publishers.

Jha, Praveen. 2005. 'Withering Commitments and Weakening Progress: State and Education in the Era of Neoliberal Reforms'. *Economic and Political Weekly* 40 (33): 3677–84.

Jones, Nicola and Andy Sumner. 2007. 'Does Mixed Methods Research Matter to Understanding Childhood Well-being?'. Wellbeing in Developing Countries (WeD) working paper no. 40, ESRC Research Group, UK.

Kainth, Gursharan Singh. 2006. 'A Mission Approach to Sarva Shiksha Abhiyan'. *Economic and Political Weekly* 41 (30), July: 3288–91.

Kannan, K. P., and G. Raveendran. 2011. 'India's Common People: The Regional Profile'. *Economic and Political Weekly* 46 (38): 60–73.

Katsillis, John and Richard Rubinson. 1990. 'Cultural Capital, Student Achievement, and Educational Reproduction: The Case of Greece'. *American Sociological Review* 55 (2): 270–79.

Kaul, Rekha. 1993. *Caste, Class and Education: Politics of the Capitation Fee Phenomenon in Karnataka*. New Delhi: Sage Publications.

Kelley, Allen C. 1991. 'The Human Development Index: "Handle with Care"'. *Population and Development Review* 17 (2): 315–24.

Ken, Ivy. 2008. 'Beyond the Intersection: A New Culinary Metaphor for Race-Class-Gender Studies'. *Sociological Theory* 26 (2): 152–72.

Khader, Serene J. 2009. 'Adaptive Preferences and Procedural Autonomy'. *Journal of Human Development and Capabilities* 10 (2): 169–87.

———. 2011. *Adaptive Preferences and Women's Empowerment*. New Delhi: Oxford University Press.

———. 2012. 'Must Theorising about Adaptive Preferences Deny Women's Agency?'. *Journal of Applied Philosophy* 29 (4): 302–17.

Kieselbach, Thomas, Cornelis Van Heeringen, Michele La Rosa, Louis Lemkow, Katerina Sokou and Bengt Starrin (eds). 2001. *Living on the Edge: An Empirical Analysis on Long-term Youth Unemployment and Social Exclusion in Europe*. Opladen, Germany: Leske and Budrich.

King, James R. 2000. 'Inconsistencies in Education and Ethnography Offer Rays of Hope'. *Journal of Contemporary Ethnography* 29 (6): 747–55.

King, Kenneth, Simon McGrath and Pauline Rose. 2007. 'Beyond the Basics: Educating and Training Out of Poverty'. *International Journal of Educational Development* 27 (4): 349–57.

Kingston, Paul W. 2001. 'The Unfulfilled Promise of Cultural Capital Theory'. *Sociology of Education* 74: 88–99.

Kothari, Uma and Martin Minogue (eds). 2002. *Development Theory and Practice: Critical Perspectives*. Basingstoke: Palgrave.

Kumar, A. K. Shiva, n.d. 'Poverty and Human Development in India: Getting Priorities Right'. Available at http://hdr.undp.org/docs/publications/ocational_papers/oc30.htm (accessed 18 November 2014).

Kumar, Krishna. 1987. 'Reproduction or Change?: Education and Elites in India'. In *Education and the Process of Change*, ed. Ratna Ghosh and Mathew Zachariah, 27–41. New Delhi: Sage Publications.

_____. 2004. 'Quality of Education at the Beginning of the 21st Century: Lessons from India'. Background paper prepared for Global Monitoring Report 2005, Education For All: The Quality Imperative, UNESCO.

_____. 2005. 'Quality Education at the Beginning of the 21st Century: Lessons from India'. Background paper prepared for Education for All Global Monitoring Report 2005, UNESCO. Available at https://unesdoc.unesco.org/ark:/48223/pf0000146663 (accessed 15 July 2013).

_____. 2007. 'EFA and the Quality Debate: Perspective from India's National Curriculum Framework, 2005'. Lecture delivered at London International Development Centre, London, 5 December.

_____. 2011. 'Teaching and the Neo-liberal State'. *Economic and Political Weekly* 46 (21): 37–40.

_____. 2014. *Politics of Education in Colonial India*. New Delhi: Routledge.

Kumar, Krishna and Padma M. Sarangapani. 2004. 'History of the Quality Debate'. Background paper prepared for the Global Monitoring Report 2005, Education For All: The Quality Imperative, UNESCO. Available at https://unesdoc.unesco.org/ark:/48223/pf0000146655_eng (accessed 15 July 2013).

Kumar, Ravi. 2000. 'Education in the Times of Extremist Violence: A Case of Rampur Chai Village in Jehanabad, Bihar'. Operation Blackboard Project: An Ethnographic Study, National Institute of Educational Planning and Administration, New Delhi.

Kumar, Sanjay, Anthony Heath and Oliver Heath. 2002. 'Determinants of Social Mobility in India'. *Economic and Political Weekly* 37 (29): 2983–87.

Laderchi, Caterina Ruggeri. 2001. 'Participatory Methods in the Analysis of Poverty: A Critical Review'. QEH working paper series QEHWPS62, Queen Elizabeth House, University of Oxford.

Lamont, James. 2011. 'India's Abject Return to Talk of Hindu Growth Rates'. *Financial Times* (Europe edition), 28 September, 11.

Lamont, Michele and Annette Lareau. 1988. 'Cultural Capital: Allusions, Gaps and Glissandos in Recent Theoretical Developments'. *Sociological Theory* 6 (2): 153–68.

Lareau, Annette. 2003. *Unequal Childhoods: Class, Race, and Family Life*. California: University of California Press.

Lareau, Annette and Erin McNamara Horvat. 1999. 'Moments of Social Inclusion and Exclusion Race, Class, and Cultural Capital in Family-School Relationships'. *Sociology of Education* 72 (1): 37–53.

Lee, Stacey J. 2007. 'Theorizing Class through Ethnography'. *Educational Researcher* 36 (1): 33–36.

Lerche, Jens. 2010. 'Agrarian Crisis and Agrarian Questions in India'. *Journal of Agrarian Change* 11 (1): 104–18.

Leßmann, Ortrud, Hans-Uwe Otto and Holger Ziegler. 2011. *Closing the Capabilities Gap: Regenerating Social Justice for the Young*. Germany: Barbara Budrich Publishers.

Levine, David P. 2004. 'Poverty, Capabilities and Freedom'. *Review of Political Economy* 16 (1): 101–15.

Lewis, O. 1998. 'The Culture of Poverty'. *Society* 35 (2): 7–9.

Lind, Niels C. 1992. 'Some Thoughts on the Human Development Index'. *Social Indicators Research* 27 (1): 89–101.

Lipsky, Michael. 1969. 'Toward a Theory of Street-level Bureaucracy'. Discussion paper no. 48–69, Institute for Research on Poverty, University of Wisconsin, Madison. Available at http://www.irp.wisc.edu/publications/dps/pdfs/dp4869.pdf (accessed 11 October 2011).

Lister, Ruth. 2009. 'A Nordic Nirvana?: Gender, Citizenship, and Social Justice in the Nordic Welfare States'. *Social Politics: International Studies in Gender, State and Society* 16 (2): 242–78.

Lofland, John. 1995. 'Analytic Ethnography: Features, Failings, and Futures'. *Journal of Contemporary Ethnography* 24 (1): 30–67.

Lutz, Helma, Maria Teresa Herrera Vivar and Linda Supik (eds). 2011. *Framing Intersectionality: Debates on a Multi-faceted Concept in Gender Studies*. UK: Ashgate Publishing.

Lykke, Nina. 2010. *Feminist Studies: A Guide to Intersectional Theory, Methodology and Writing*. New York: Routledge.

Lyon, Eleanor. 1999. 'Reflections on the Future of Applied Ethnography'. *Journal of Contemporary Ethnography* 28 (6): 620–27.

Mach, Bogdan W., and Wlodzimierz Wesolowski. 1986. *Social Mobility and Social Structure*, trans. Barbara Zawadzka. London: Routledge and Kegan Paul.

Madan, T. N. 1975. 'On Living Intimately with Strangers'. In *Encounters and Experience: Personal Accountants of Fieldwork*, ed. André Béteille and T. N. Madan, 149. New Delhi: Vikas.

———. 1984. Review of '*Rural Society in Southeast India* by Kathleen Gough'. *American Ethnologist* 11 (2): 388–90.

Madan, T. N. 1998. 'Discovering Anthropology: A Personal Narrative'. In *Anthropological Journeys: Reflections on Fieldwork*, ed. Meenakshi Thapan, 143–62. New Delhi: Orient Longman.

MacDonald, Robert (ed.). 1997. *Youth, the 'Underclass' and Social Exclusion*. London: Routledge.

Maertens, Annemie. 2011. 'Does Education Pay Off?: Subjective Expectations on Education in Rural India'. *Economic and Political Weekly* 46 (9): 58–63.

Mander, Harsh. 2010. '"Words from the Heart": Researching People's Stories'. *Journal of Human Rights Practice* 2 (2): 252–70.

Mangalam, J. J. 1965. Review of '*When Caste Barriers Fall: A Study of Social and Economic Change in a South Indian Village* by Dagfinn Sivertsen'. *Social Forces* 43 (4): 622–23.

Mann, Michael. 1983. *Macmillan Student Encyclopedia of Sociology*. London: Macmillan.

Marnane, Patrick J. H. 1967. 'Individual Social Mobility in India'. *Sociological Bulletin* 16 (2): 60–66.

Max-Neef, M. 1991. *Human Scale Development: Conception, Application and Further Reflections*. New York: Apex Press.

Maxwell, James D., and Mary Percival Maswell. 1995. 'The Reproduction of Class in Canada's Elite Independent Schools'. *British Journal of Sociology of Education* 16 (3): 309–26.

McGillivray, Mark. 1991. 'The Human Development Index: Yet Another Redundant Composite Development Indicator?'. *World Development* 19 (10): 1461–68.

Mehrotra, Santosh and Peter Buckland. 2001. 'Managing School Teacher Costs for Access and Quality in Developing Countries'. *Economic and Political Weekly* 36 (49): 4567–79.

Mehrotra, Santosh. 2005. 'Human Capital or Human Development?: Search for a Knowledge Paradigm for Education and Development'. *Economic and Political Weekly* 40 (4): 300–06.

Mencher, Joan P. 1970. 'A Tamil Village: Changing Socioeconomic Structure in Madras State'. In *Change and Continuity in India's Villages*, ed. K. Ishwaran, 197–218. New York: Columbia University Press.

Mendelsohn, Oliver and Marika Vicziany. 1998. *The Untouchables: Subordination, Poverty and the State in Modern India*. Cambridge: Cambridge University Press.

Migheli, Matteo. 2011. 'Capabilities and Functionings: The Role of Social Capital for Accessing New Capabilities'. *Review of Political Economy* 23 (1): 133–42.

Miller, Gale. 1994. 'Toward Ethnographies of Institutional Discourse: Proposal and Suggestions'. *Journal of Contemporary Ethnography* 23 (3): 280–306.

Mitra, Sanjay and Shashi Kant Verma. 1997. 'Why Governments Devolve: A Study Using Data from Indian States'. Development Discussion paper no. 586, Harvard Institute for International Development.

Myrdal, Gunnar. 1974. 'What Is Development?'. *Journal of Economic Issues* 8 (4): 729–36.

Nabokov, Isabelle. 2000. 'Deadly Power: A Funeral to Counter Sorcery in South India'. *American Ethnologist* 27 (1): 147–68.

Naik, J. P. 1979. 'Equality, Quality and Quantity: The Elusive Triangle in Indian Education'. *International Review of Education* 25 (2–3): 167–85.

Nambissan, Geetha B. 2000. 'Dealing with Deprivation'. *Seminar* 493. Available at https://www.india-seminar.com/2000/493/493%20geetha%20b.%20nambissan.htm (accessed 18 November 2010).

Nandy, Santosh Kumar. 1966. Review of '*Caste, Class, and Power: Changing Patterns of Stratification in a Tanjore Village* by André Béteille'. *American Sociological Review* 31 (5): 729–30.

National Council of Educational Research and Training. 2005. National Curriculum Framework 2005, New Delhi.

Nicholas, Ralph W. 1966. Review of '*Caste, Class, and Power: Changing Patterns of Stratification in a Tanjore Village* by André Béteille'. *The Journal of Asian Studies* 26 (1): 139–40.

Nussbaum, Martha C. 2006. 'Education and Democratic Citizenship: Capabilities and Quality Education'. *Journal of Human Development* 7 (3): 385–95.

———. 2010. *Not for Profit: Why Democracy Needs the Humanities*. New Jersey: Princeton University Press.

———. 2011. *Creating Capabilities: The Human Development Approach*. US: Harvard University Press.

Nutrition Foundation of India. 2003. 'A Report of the Workshop on Mid-day Meal Programmes in Schools in India: The Way Forward'. New Delhi.

Ogbu, John U. 1981. 'School Ethnography: A Multilevel Approach'. *Anthropology and Education Quarterly*, Issues in School Ethnography 12 (1): 3–29.

Omvedt, Gail. 2003. 'Caste and Hinduism'. *Economic and Political Weekly* 38 (47): 5003–04.

———. 2004. 'Caste System and Hinduism'. *Economic and Political Weekly* 39 (11): 1179–80.

Otto, Hans-Uwe and Holger Ziegler. 2013. *Enhancing Capabilities: The Role of Social Institutions*. Germany: Barbara Budrich.

Pal, Shukti. 2000. 'A Case of Jatrapur Bhootpara Adivasi Primary School in West Bengal'. Operation Blackboard Project: An Ethnographic Study, National Institute of Educational Planning and Administration, New Delhi.

Pandian, M. S. S. 2008. 'Writing Ordinary Lives'. *Economic and Political Weekly* 43 (38): 34–40.

Panikkar, K. N. 2011. 'India's Education Policy: From National to Commercial'. *Economic and Political Weekly* 46 (17): 38–42.

Paranjape, Madhu S. 2007. 'Uneven Distribution of Education in Maharashtra: Rural-Urban, Gender and Caste Inequalities'. *Economic and Political Weekly* 42 (3), 20–26 January: 213–16.

Pastrana, Jr., Antonio. 2004. 'Black Identity Constructions: Inserting Intersectionality, Bisexuality, and (Afro-) Latinidad into Black Studies'. *Journal of African American Studies* 8 (1–2): 74–89.

Pathak, Avijit. 2002. *Social Implications of Schooling: Knowledge, Pedagogy and Consciousness*. Delhi: Rainbow Publishers.

Pathy, Suguna. 2003. 'Destitution, Deprivation and Tribal "Development"'. *Economic and Political Weekly* 38 (27): 2832–36.

Pattenden, Jonathan. 2011. 'Social Protection and Class Relations: Evidence from Scheduled Caste Women's Associations in Rural South India'. *Development and Change* 42 (2): 469–98.

Prasenjit, Maiti. 2003. 'School Children are Hungry in India'. Available at http://www.boloji.com/analysis/063.htm (accessed 20 April 2013).

Preissle, Judith and Linda Grant. 1998. 'Exploring the Ethnography of Education'. *Journal of Contemporary Ethnography* 27 (1): 3–9.

PROBE Team. 1999. *Public Report on Basic Education in India*. New Delhi: Oxford University Press.

Purdie-Vaughns, Valerie and Richard P. Eibach. 2008. 'Intersectional Invisibility: The Distinctive Advantages and Disadvantages of Multiple Subordinate-group Identities'. *Sex Roles* 59 (5): 377–91.

Raina, Vinod. 2002. 'Decentralisation of Education'. In *India Education Report: A Profile of Basic Education*, ed. R. Govinda, 111–20. New Delhi: Oxford University Press.

Ramachandran, Vimala, Jitender Sharma, Madhumita Pal and Sharada Jain. 2005. *Teacher Motivation in India*. New Delhi: Educational Resource Unit.

Ramkumar, N. 2000. 'A Primary School in a Rural Urban Divide: A Case of Srirampura, Karnataka State'. Operation Blackboard Project: An Ethnographic Study, National Institute of Educational Planning and Administration, New Delhi.

Rampal, Anita. 2000. 'Education for Human Development in South Asia'. *Economic and Political Weekly* 35 (30): 2523–31.

_____. 2004. 'Unpacking the "Quality" of Schools'. *Seminar* 536. Available at https://www.india-seminar.com/semframe.html (accessed 2 April 2014).

Raza, Moonis, Aijazuddin Ahmad and Sheel C. Nuna. 1990. *School Education in India: The Regional Dimension*. New Delhi: NIEPA.

Reader, Soran. 2006. 'Does a Basic Needs Approach Need Capabilities'. *The Journal of Political Philosophy* 14 (3): 337–50.

Robertson, David. 1993. 'The Penguin Dictionary of Politics'. England: Penguin Books.

Robertson, Susan L., Lois Weis and Fazal Rizvi. 2011. 'The Global Auction: The Broken Promises of Education, Jobs and Incomes'. *British Journal of Sociology of Education* 32 (2): 293–311.

Robeyns, Ingrid. 2000. 'An Unworkable Idea or a Promising Alternative?: Sen's Capabilities Approach Re-examined'. Discussion Paper Series, Ku Leuven. Available at http://www.econ.kuleuven.be/ces/discssionpapers/default.htm (accessed 31 August 2012).

———. 2005. 'The Capabilities Approach: A Theoretical Survey'. *Journal of Human Development* 6 (1): 93–114.

———. 2006. 'Three Models of Education: Rights, Capabilities and Human Capital'. *Theory and Research in Education* 4 (1): 69–84.

Rogers, Rebecca, Elizabeth Malancharuvil-Berkes, Melissa Mosley, Diane Hui and Glynis O'Garro Joseph. 2005. 'Critical Discourse Analysis in Education: A Review of the Literature'. *Review of Educational Research* 75 (3): 365–416.

Rolnick, Phyllis J. 1965. Review of '*When Caste Barriers Fall: A Study of Social and Economic Change in a South Indian Village* by Dagfinn Sivertsen'. *American Journal of Sociology*, 71 (2): 223–24.

Rose, Pauline and Caroline Dyer. 2006. 'Chronic Poverty and Education: A Review of the Literature'. Background paper for the 2007 Chronic Poverty Report, Overseas Development Institute, London.

Roy, Dayabati. 2008. 'Whither the Subaltern Domain?: An Ethnographic Enquiry'. *Economic and Political Weekly* 43 (23): 31–38.

Rustagi, Preet (ed.). 2009. *Concerns, Conflicts and Cohesions: Universalization of Elementary Education in India*. New Delhi: Oxford University Press.

Sainath, P. 2001. 'Hero by Name and Deed'. *The Hindu*, New Delhi, 21 January.

Saith, Ashwani and Rekha Wazir. 2009. 'From Poverty to Wellbeing: Alternative Approaches to the Recognition of Child Deprivation in India'. Background paper for Institute of Human Development, UNICEF India Country Report on Child Poverty and Disparities.

Saith, Ruhi. 2001. 'Capabilities: The Concept and its Operationalisation'. QEH working paper no. 66, Queen Elizabeth House, University of Oxford.

Saito, Madoka. 2003. 'Amartya Sen's Capabilities Approach to Education: A Critical Exploration'. *Journal of Philosophy of Education* 37 (1): 17–33.

Sanders, Clinton R. 1999. 'Prospects for a Post-modern Ethnography'. *Journal of Contemporary Ethnography* 28 (6): 669–75.

Sarangapani, Padma M. 2003. *Constructing School Knowledge: An Ethnography of Learning in an Indian Village*. New Delhi: Sage Publications.

Schultz, Theodore W. 1961. 'Investment in Human Capital'. *The American Economic Review* 51 (1): 1–17.

_____. 1962. 'Reflections on Investment in Man'. *The Journal of Political Economy* 70 (5), Part 2: 1–8.

Scott, Susie. 2010. 'Revisiting the Total Institution: Performative Regulation in the Reinventive Institution'. *Sociology* 44 (2): 213–31.

Selwyn, Ben. 2011. 'Liberty Limited?: A Sympathetic Re-engagement with Amartya Sen's *Development as Freedom*'. *Economic and Political Weekly* 46 (37): 68–76.

Sen, Amartya. 1973. 'Poverty, Inequality and Unemployment: Some Conceptual Issues in Measurement'. *Economic and Political Weekly* 8 (31–33): 1457–64.

_____. 1976. 'Famines as Failures of Exchange Entitlements'. *Economic and Political Weekly* 11 (31–33): 1273–80.

_____. 1980. 'Famines'. *World Development* 8 (9): 613–21.

_____. 1981. 'Ingredients of Famine Analysis: Availability and Entitlements'. *The Quarterly Journal of Economics* 96 (3): 433–64.

_____. 1983. 'Development: Which Way Now?'. *The Economic Journal* 93 (372): 745–62.

_____. 1986. 'Food, Economics and Entitlements'. Working paper no. 1, World Institute for Development Economics Research, United Nations University.

_____. 1987. 'Research for Action: Hunger and Entitlements'. Conference paper, World Institute for Development Economics Research, United Nations University.

_____. 1997. 'Human Capital and Human Capability'. *World Development* 25 (12): 1959–61.

_____. 1999a. *Commodities and Capabilities*. New Delhi: Oxford University Press.

_____. 1999b. *Development as Freedom*. Delhi: Oxford University Press.

_____. 1999c. 'Poverty as Capability Deprivation'. In *Development As Freedom*, 87–110. New Delhi: Oxford University Press.

_____. 2000. 'A Decade of Human Development'. *Journal of Human Development* 1 (1): 17–23.

_____. 2004. 'Capabilities, Lists and Public Reason: Continuing the Conversation'. *Feminist Economics* 10 (3): 77–80.

_____. 2005. 'How Does Development Happen?'. *Cato Journal* 25 (3): 455–59.

_____. 2009. *The Idea of Justice*. Cambridge: Harvard University Press.

Sengupta, Arjun, G. Raveendran and K. P. Kannan. 2008. 'India's Common People: Who Are They, How Many Are They and How Do They Live?'. *Economic and Political Weekly* 43 (11): 49-63.

Sengupta, Mitu. 2008. 'How the State Changed Its Mind: Power, Politics and the Origins of India's Market Reforms'. *Economic and Political Weekly* 43 (21): 35–42.

Sharma, Jyotirmoyee. 1967. Review of '*Caste, Class, and Power: Changing Patterns of Stratification in a Tanjore Village* by André Béteille, and *Tradition and Economy in Village India* by K. Ishwaran'. *Man* 2 (1): 152.

Sharma, K. L. 1973. 'Downward Social Mobility: Some Observations'. *Sociological Bulletin* 22 (1): 59–77.

Shaw, John. 2006. 'Hans Wolfgang Singer'. In *Fifty Key Thinkers on Development*, ed. David Simon, 242–47. New York: Routledge.

Shields, Stephanic A. 2008. 'Gender: An Intersectionality Perspective'. *Sex Roles* 59 (5): 301–11.

Singh, Avinash Kumar. 1995. 'The Cultural Construction of Home and School Knowledge in Tribal India'. *Prospects* 25 (4): 735–47.

Sinha, Murli M. 1973. Review of '*Caste, Class, and Power: Changing Patterns of Stratification in a Tanjore Village* by André Béteille'. *Contemporary Sociology: A Journal of Reviews* 2 (3): 294.

Sivertsen, Dagfinn. 1963. *When Caste Barriers Fall: A Study of Social and Economic Change in a South Indian Village*. Oslo and New York: Universitetsforlaget and Humanities Press.

Solanke, Iyiola. 2009. 'Putting Race and Gender Together: A New Approach to Intersectionality'. *The Modern Law Review* 72 (5): 723–49.

Srinivas, M. N. 1955. 'The Social System of a Mysore Village'. In *Village India: Studies in the Little Community*, ed. McKim Marriott, 1–35. Chicago: University of Chicago Press.

———. 1987. *The Dominant Caste and Other Essays*. New Delhi: Oxford University Press.

———. 1997. 'Practicing Social Anthropology in India'. *Annual Review of Anthropology* 26: 1–24.

———. 2004. 'The Insider versus the Outsider in the Study of Cultures'. In *Methodology and Fieldwork*, ed. Vinay Kumar Srivastava, 413–20. New Delhi: Oxford University Press.

———. 2009. *The Oxford India Srinivas*. New Delhi: Oxford University Press.

———. 2010. *The Remembered Village* (seventh impression). New Delhi: Oxford University Press.

Srinivasan, T. N. 1994. 'Human Development: A New Paradigm or Reinvention of the Wheel?'. *The American Economic Review* 84 (2): 238–43.

Srivastava, Vinay Kumar (ed.). 1991a. 'The Ethnographer and the People: Reflections on Field Work'. *Economic and Political Weekly* 26 (22–23): 1408–14.

_____. 1991b. 'The Ethnographer and the People: Reflections on Field Work'. *Economic and Political Weekly* 26 (24): 1475–81.

_____. 1999. 'The Future of Anthropology'. *Economic and Political Weekly* 34 (9): 545–52.

_____. 2004. *Methodology and Fieldwork*. New Delhi: Oxford University Press.

Stanley, Liz. 1990. 'Doing Ethnography, Writing Ethnography: A Comment on Hammersley'. *Sociology* 24 (4): 617–27.

Stewart, Frances. 1980. 'Country Experience in Providing for Basic Needs'. In *Poverty and Basic Needs*, 9–12. Washington, DC: World Bank.

Still, Clarinda. 2011. 'Spoiled Brides and the Fear of Education: Honour and Social Mobility among Dalits in South India'. *Modern Asian Studies* 45 (5): 1119–46.

Stoddart, Kenneth. 1986. 'The Presentation of Everyday Life: Some Textual Strategies for "Adequate Ethnography"'. *Urban Life* 15 (1): 103–21.

Støren, Liv Anne and Per Olaf Aamodt. 2010. 'The Quality of Higher Education and Employability of Graduates'. *Quality in Higher Education* 16 (3): 297–313.

Streeten, Paul. 1971. 'Basic Human Needs'. *Millennium: Journal of International Studies* 1 (1): 29–46.

_____. 1994. 'Human Development: Means and Ends'. *The American Economic Review* 84 (2): 232–37.

Streeten, Paul and Shahid Javed Burki. 1978. 'Basic Needs: Some Issues'. *World Development* 6 (3): 411–21.

Strickland, Ronald. 2005. 'Nothing that is Human Alien to Me: Neoliberalism and the End of *Bildung*'. *Review of Literatures of the European Union* 1: 29–40.

Sullivan, Alice. 2001. 'Cultural Capital and Educational Attainment'. *Sociology* 35 (4): 893–912.

Surti, Tehzeeb and Nandini Majrekar. 2000. 'Schooling on the Margins of Development: A Study in Kathifarya Shivrajpur, Panchmahals District, Gujarat'. Operation Blackboard Project: An Ethnographic Study, National Institute of Educational Planning and Administration, New Delhi.

Swaminathan, Padmini, J. Jeyaranjan, R. Sreenivasan and K. Jayashree. 2004. 'Tamil Nadu's Midday Meal Scheme: Where Assumed Benefits Score over Hard Data'. *Economic and Political Weekly* 39 (44): 4811–21.

Sweeney, Jackie and Lucy Naish. 2001. '"We Can Think But We Can't Do." Does Increased Education Lead to Greater Autonomy for Women?:

The Aspirations of Young Female College Students in Coimbatore'. Southern India and Societal Constraints, Edinburgh Papers in South Asian Studies no. 15, Centre for South Asian Studies, School of Social and Political Studies, University of Edinburgh.

Sweetland, Scott R. 1996. 'Human Capital Theory: Foundations of a Field of Inquiry'. *Review of Educational Research* 66 (3): 341–59.

Talib, Mohammad. 1992. 'Ideology, Curriculum and Class Construction: Observations from A School in a Working Class Settlement in Delhi'. *Sociological Bulletin* 41 (1–2): 81–95.

Taylor, Yvette, Sally Hines and Mark E. Casey (eds). 2010. *Theorizing Intersectionality and Sexuality*. UK: Palgrave Macmillan.

Teachman, Jay D. 1987. 'Family Background, Educational Resources, and Educational Attainment'. *American Sociological Review* 52 (4): 548–57.

Terzi, Lorella. 2007. 'Capability and Educational Equality: The Just Distribution of Resources to Students with Disabilities and Special Education Needs'. *Journal of Philosophy of Education* 41 (4): 757–73.

Teschl, M., and F. Comim. 2005. 'Adaptive Preferences and Capabilities: Some Preliminary Conceptual Explorations'. *Review of Social Economy* 63 (2): 229–47.

Thapan, Meenakshi. 1984. 'Education and Ideology: The School as a Socio-cultural System'. PhD thesis, University of Delhi.

———. 2009. *Life at School: An Ethnographic Study* (second edition). New Delhi: Oxford University Press.

Thorat, Amit. 2010. 'Ethnicity, Caste and Religion: Implications for Poverty Outcomes'. *Economic and Political Weekly* 45 (51): 47–53.

Thorat, Sukhdeo. 2005. 'Reservation and Efficiency: Myth and Reality'. *Economic and Political Weekly* 40 (9): 808–10.

———. 2007. 'Human Poverty and Socially Disadvantaged Groups in India'. Discussion Paper Series 18, Human Development Resource Centre, UNDP, India.

Thorat, Sukhdeo and Joel Lee. 2005. 'Caste Discrimination and Food Security Programmes'. *Economic and Political Weekly* 40 (39): 4198–4201.

Thorat, Sukhdeo and Katherine S. Newman. 2007. 'Caste and Economic Discrimination: Causes, Consequences and Remedies'. *Economic and Political Weekly* 42 (41): 4121–24.

Tilak, J. B. G. 1999. 'Education and Poverty in South Asia'. *Prospects: Quarterly Review of Comparative Education* 29 (4): 517–33.

———. 2002a. 'Education and Poverty'. *Journal of Human Development* 3 (2): 191–207.

———. 2002b. 'Education Poverty in India'. *Review of Development and Change* 7 (1): 1–44.

Tilak, J. B. G. 2003. 'Privatisation of Higher Education'. In *Education, Society and Development: National and International Perspectives*, ed. J. B. G. Tilak, 557–74. New Delhi: APH Publishing Corporation.

_____. 2005. 'Post-elementary Education, Poverty and Development in India'. Paper presented at the 8th UKFIET Oxford International Conference on Education and Development: Learning and Livelihoods, University of Oxford, 13–15 September 2005.

_____. 2007. 'Post-elementary Education, Poverty and Development in India'. *International Journal of Educational Development* 27: 435–45.

Tomlinson, Michael. 2008. '"The Degree is Not Enough": Students' Perceptions of the Role of Higher Education Credentials for Graduate Work and Employability'. *British Journal of Sociology of Education* 29 (1): 49–61.

Tooley, James. 2004. 'Could Globalisation of Education Benefit the Poor?'. Occasional paper no. 3, Liberal Institute of the Friedrich Naumann Foundation, Berlin.

Tooley, James and Pauline Dixon. 2007. 'Private Schooling for Low-income Families: A Census and Comparative Survey in East Delhi, India'. *International Journal of Educational Development* 27: 205–19.

Townsend, Peter. 1954. 'Measuring Poverty'. *The British Journal of Sociology* 5 (2): 130–37.

Trabold-Nübler, Harald. 1991. 'The Human Development Index: A New Development Indicator'. *Intereconomics* 26 (5): 236–43.

Trujillo, Nick. 1999. 'Teaching Ethnography in the Twenty-first Century Using Collaborative Learning'. *Journal of Contemporary Ethnography* 28 (6): 705–19.

Tyagi, Anjula. 2000. 'Primary Education: On the Criterion of Reality, A Case of Dhaki Village (Uttar Pradesh)'. Operation Blackboard Project: An Ethnographic Study, National Institute of Educational Planning and Administration, New Delhi.

UNICEF. 2000. 'Defining Quality in Education'. Working Paper Series, Education Division, UNICEF, US, paper presented at the meeting of The International Working Group on Education, at Florence, Italy, June.

Unterhalter, Elaine. 2003a. 'Crossing Disciplinary Boundaries: The Potential of Sen's Capabilities Approach for Sociologists of Education'. *British Journal of Sociology of Education* 24 (5): 665–69.

_____. 2003b. 'Education, Capabilities and Social Justice'. Background paper prepared for the Education for All Global Monitoring Report 2003/4—Gender and Education for All: The Leap to Equality, UNESCO.

_____. 2013. 'Educating Capabilities'. *Journal of Human Development and Capabilities* 14 (1): 185–88.

Upadhya, Carol. 2007. 'Employment, Exclusion and "Merit" in the Indian IT Industry'. *Economic and Political Weekly* 42 (20): 1863–68.

Varghese, N. V. 1989. 'Education and the Labour Market in India'. IIEP Research Report 67, International Institute for Educational Planning, Paris.

——— (ed.). 1997. 'Educational Planning at the District Level: Meaning and Scope'. In *Modules on District Planning in Education*. New Delhi: National Institute of Educational Planning and Administration.

———. 2008. 'State is the Problem and State is the Solution: The Changing Orientations in Educational Planning'. Directions in Educational Planning: Symposium to Honour the work of Francoise Caillods, International Institute for Educational Planning, Paris.

Vasavi, A. R. 2009. 'New Imperatives for Elementary Education'. *Indian Journal of Human Development* 3 (1): 133–42.

Velaskar, Padma. 1990. 'Unequal Schooling as a Factor in the Reproduction of Social Inequality in India'. *Sociological Bulletin* 39 (1–2): 131–45.

———. 2010. 'Quality and Inequality in Indian Education: Some Critical Policy Concerns'. *Contemporary Education Dialogue* 7 (1): 58–93.

Venkataraman, L. N. 2011. 'False Consciousness'. *Economic and Political Weekly* 44 (22): 4.

———. 2013. 'Quality, Employability and Capabilities: The Enduring Elusive Triangle in Indian Education'. *ASIEN: The German Journal on Contemporary Asia* 127, April: S30–47.

———. 2014a. 'Caste, Class and Education: The Intersectional Implications of Capabilities Formation in a South Indian Village'. In *New Approaches Towards the Good Life: Applications and Transformations of the Capability Approach*, ed. Otto Schäfer, 107–121. Germany: Barbara Budrich Publishers.

———. 2014b. 'Caste and the Mainstream Narratives'. *Economic and Political Weekly* 49 (6): 76–77.

———. 2014c. 'Orphan-schooling in India: A Reflexive Account from Sripuram'. *Sociological Bulletin: Journal of the Indian Sociological Society* 63 (2): 302–13.

———. 2015. 'Social Construction of Capabilities and Intersectional Complexities in a Tamil Village'. *Development in Practice* 25 (8): 1170–81.

———. 2016a. 'New Education Policy and the Continuing Contentions in India'. *Economic and Political Weekly* 51 (35): 47–50.

———. 2016b. 'Social Sciences in India: Premises and Promises of Capability Approach'. *Indian Journal of Human Development* 10 (1): 1–11.

———. 2018a. 'Can Lateral Entry in the IAS Ensure Good Governance?'. *Economic and Political Weekly* 53 (32): 1–6.

Venkataraman, L. N. 2018b. 'Capitals and Capabilities: Social Reproduction of Inequalities in Sripuram'. In *Youth, Gender and the Capabilities Approach to Development: Rethinking Opportunities and Agency from a Human Development Perspective*, ed. Aurora Lopez-Fogues and Firdevs Melis Cin, 92–107. London and New York: Routledge.

_____. 2018c. 'The Privatisation of Public Welfare in India'. *Social Work and Society* 16 (2): 1–5.

_____. 2019. 'Publication or Public Action?: Discursive Spaces of Disengagements in India'. In *Education and the Public Sphere: Exploring the Structures of Mediation in Post-colonial India*, ed. G. S. Suresh Babu, 93–105. UK: Routledge.

Verloo, Mieke. 2006. 'Multiple Inequalities, Intersectionality and the European Union'. *European Journal of Women's Studies* 13 (3): 211–28.

Viswanathan, Brinda. 2006. 'Access to Nutritious Meal Programmes: Evidence from 1999–2000 NSS Data'. *Economic and Political Weekly* 41 (6): 497–505.

von Wright, Moira. 2002. 'Narrative Imagination and Taking the Perspective of Others'. *Studies in Philosophy and Education* 21 (4): 407–16.

Wagner, Jon. 1993. 'Ignorance in Educational Research: Or, How Can You "Not" Know That?'. *Educational Researcher* 22 (5): 15–23.

Walford, Geoffrey (ed.). 2001. *Ethnography and Education Policy*. UK: Elsevier Science Ltd.

Walker, Melanie and Elaine Unterhalter (eds). 2007. *Amartya Sen's Capabilities Approach and Social Justice in Education*. New York: Palgrave Macmillan.

Walker, Melanie. 2003. 'Framing Social Justice in Education: What Does the "Capabilities" Approach Offer?'. *British Journal of Educational Studies* 51 (2): 168–87.

_____. 2006. 'Towards a Capability-based Theory of Social Justice for Education Policy-making'. *Journal of Education Policy* 21 (2): 163–85.

_____. 2010. 'Critical Capability Pedagogies and University Education'. *Educational Philosophy and Theory* 42 (8): 898–917.

_____. 2012. 'Introduction'. *Journal of Human Development and Capabilities* 13 (3): 331–34.

Wankhede, G. G. 2001. 'Educational Inequalities among Scheduled Castes in Maharashtra'. *Economic and Political Weekly* 36 (18): 1553–58.

Washbrook, D. A. 1983. Review of '*Rural Society in Southeast India* by Kathleen Gough'. *Pacific Affairs* 56 (3): 565–67.

Watts, Michael. 2013. 'The Complexities of Adaptive Preferences in Post-compulsory Education: Insights from the Fable of the Fox and the Grapes'. *Journal of Human Development and Capabilities* 14 (4): 503–19.

Weiner, Myron. 1991. 'The Child and the State in India: Child Labor and Education Policy in Comparative Perspective'. New Delhi: Oxford University Press.

Weisskopf, Thomas E. 2004. *Affirmative Action in the United States and India: A Comparative Perspective*. London: Routledge.

——. 2011. 'Why Worry about Inequality in the Booming Indian Economy'. *Economic and Political Weekly* 46 (47): 41–51.

Wheeler, David. 1980. 'Basic Needs Fulfillment and Economic Growth: A Simultaneous Model'. *Journal of Development Economics* 7 (4): 435–51.

Whitaker, Mark P. 1996. 'Ethnography as Learning: A Wittgensteinian Approach to Writing Ethnographic Accounts'. *Anthropological Quarterly* 69 (1): 1–13.

White, Howard, Jennifer Leavy and Andrew Masters. 2003. 'Comparative Perspective on Child Poverty: A Review of Poverty Measures'. *Journal of Human Development* 4 (3): 379–96.

Whyte, W. F. 1967. *Street Corner Society: The Social Structure of an Italian Slum*, eleventh impression. US: The University of Chicago Press.

Willims, J. Douglas and Alan C. Kerchoff. 1995. 'The Challenge of Developing New Educational Indicators'. *Educational Evaluation and Policy Analysis* 17 (1): 113–31.

Willis, Paul and Mats Trondman. 2000. 'Manifesto for "Ethnography"'. *Ethnography* 1 (1): 5–16.

Willis, Paul. 1977. *Learning to Labour: How Working Class Kids Get Working Class Jobs*. New York: Columbia University Press.

Winker, Gabriele and Nina Degele. 2011. 'Intersectionality as Multi-level Analysis: Dealing with Social Inequality'. *European Journal of Women's Studies* 18 (1): 51–66.

Wolff, Jonathan and Avner de-Shalit. 2007. *Disadvantage*. New York: Oxford University Press.

Young, Marion. 2009. 'Basic Capabilities, Basic Learning Outcomes and Thresholds of Learning'. *Journal of Human Development and Capabilities* 10 (2): 259–77.

Zaidi, Annie. 2007. 'Food, For Education'. *Frontline* 22 (5). Available at http://www.frontlineonnet.com/fl2205/stories/20050311000704900.htm (accessed 18 July 2007).

Zajda, Joseph. 2002. 'Education and Policy: Changing Paradigms and Issues'. *International Review of Education* 48 (1–2): 67–91.

Zimmermann, Benedicte. 2006. 'Pragmatism and the Capabilities Approach: Challenges in Social Theory and Empirical Research'. *European Journal of Social Theory* 9 (4): 467–84.

INDEX